Oliver Goldsmith, Thomas Gray

Goldsmith's Traveller; and Gray's Elegy in a Country Church-Yard

With Lives, Notes and Examination Questions

Oliver Goldsmith, Thomas Gray

Goldsmith's Traveller; and Gray's Elegy in a Country Church-Yard
With Lives, Notes and Examination Questions

ISBN/EAN: 9783337208837

Printed in Europe, USA, Canada, Australia, Japan

Cover: Foto ©Thomas Meinert / pixelio.de

More available books at **www.hansebooks.com**

GOLDSMITH'S
TRAVELLER

AND

GRAY'S ELEGY

IN A

COUNTRY CHURCH-YARD;

WITH

LIVES, NOTES AND EXAMINATION QUESTIONS,

BY

WILLIAM WILLIAMS, B.A.,

HEAD MASTER, COLLINGWOOD COLLEGIATE INSTITUTE,

AND

JOHN TAIT,

FIRST ENGLISH MASTER.

For the use of Graduates preparing for University Matriculation, First and second Class Teachers' Certificates, and the High School Intermediate Examination.

Toronto:
CANADA PUBLISHING COMPANY
(LIMITED).
1879.

CONTENTS.

	PAGE.
GENERAL INTRODUCTION,	v
CHRONOLOGICAL PARALLEL,	xiv
LIFE OF GOLDSMITH,	1
INTRODUCTION TO THE "TRAVELLER",	19
DEDICATION OF THE "TRAVELLER",	23
THE "TRAVELLER",	25
PRELIMINARY NOTES,	43
NOTES ON THE "TRAVELLER",	45
LIFE OF GRAY,	77
INTRODUCTION TO THE "ELEGY",	89
THE "ELEGY",	93
NOTES ON THE "ELEGY",	99
QUESTIONS FOR EXAMINATION,	129

GENERAL INTRODUCTION

The poet reflects his age. Its modes of thought, its prevailing sentiments, its tastes, are all faithfully mirrored in his writings. He is the most sensitive of men. These things make a deeper impression upon him than upon others. Though looking to future ages for the applause which the present may deny, yet he cannot afford to overlook that present, and so, writes what the public taste of the day most highly appreciates. Hence, his utterances are always deeply colored by the prevalent opinions of the time, moulded by the spirit of the age, and modified by its dominant tendencies. For this reason, we have the so-called schools of poetry, as the natural school of Chaucer, the artificial school of Pope, the romantic school of Scott and Byron, and the present school of which Tennyson and Browning are the chief representatives.

In view of the intimate connection between the poet and his age, and of the influence which they reciprocally exert upon each other, it is essential to the intelligent appreciation of his productions, to have some acquaintance with the times in which he lived. To assist the student in this respect is the object of the present chapter.

Chaucer, the great father of English poetry, was the acknowledged inventor of the English heroic line. This measure, so well adapted to the genius of the language, speedily became the favorite verse, and each succeeding poet and poetaster attempted to add something towards perfecting this accentual form of versification. To its improved regularity and more settled number of syllables, rhyme was added in imitation of the poetical forms of the Romanesque dialects; and, subsequently, when French models became the admiration of English poets, the rhyming couplet, for a time, supplanted every other form of verse. The gradually improving regularity and polish of the line are especially perceptible in the foremost poets of the language. Shakespeare greatly excels Chaucer, particularly in the number of syllables, and Milton is still more regular than Shakespeare. Dryden represents the period of transition. In his verses are the "last examples of nobleness, freedom, variety of pause and cadence, and the first models of the neatness and precision which the following generation esteemed so highly." The task of perfecting the fashion thus introduced by this great poet, was bequeathed to Pope and his school. In their poems we have art in its perfection. Correct diction, faultless versification, and mechanical brilliancy are the distinctive characteristics of the poetry of this artificial school. But, if poetry was thus brought to perfection in its mechanical structure, the great change which it underwent stripped it of some of its native charms.

A prominent feature of earlier English poetry was its love for external nature and the realities of life. In the verse of Chaucer, there breathe a freshness, vigor, and naturalness, which for some generations continued to pervade poetical literature. The period of comparative literary barrenness which followed the outburst of activity in the enterprising age of Edward the Third, was in many respects collecting forces for the unparalleled splendor of the age of Elizabeth. The revival of classical learning lent a coloring that blended not unsuitably with the spirit of our literature and gave to its entire character, elevation and polish. But it was improved, not changed. The same genuine love of nature breathes throughout the poems of our Marlowes, Greenes, Spensers, and in the writings of the 'myriad-minded' Shakespeare himself, that pervades the *Vision of Pier's Plowman* and the *Canterbury Tales*. In after years, though the Puritans banished the theatre and every vestige of imagination from the land, yet, strange to say, it was among the poets of these very people, that the love of nature still continued to struggle for life, and found in the poetry of the immortal Milton himself, its sweetest and tenderest expression.

But, by the side of the school of poetry to which Chaucer, Shakespeare, and Milton belong, there had been growing up another, distinguishable from it by drawing its informing spirit from the study of Greek and Roman classical models, as the former had derived its inspiration from the Gothic and Romance Literature of the Middle Ages. Its beginnings may be traced in the works of such English poets as Marston, Davies, and Hall, while its development becomes clearly apparent in the dramas of Ben Jonson. This classical tendency received a new impulse from the tide of French influence which flowed in upon the country, at the time of the Restoration. The school of French poetry then in vogue, had been, like that of which we have been speaking, founded upon classical models; and the popularity which it now attained in England through the influence of the court of Charles the Second, united with the English taste for classical subjects and modes of treatment then becoming fashionable; and the result of this union was to give this form of poetry so great prominence, that for some generations, it held undivided empire over the poetical taste of the country. It was under the hand of Dryden that this school of poetry rose, in some respects, to its highest eminence. But, in its mechanical perfection, its neatness and correctness, not to mention its coldness and thorough artificiality, the work which he had begun, was committed to his successor, Pope, who carried it to so great an extreme that it began to pall upon the public taste. The mechanical part of poetry may be regarded as having been now in all respects as highly polished as it was possible to make it. To so great an extent was this carried that it was at last thought that the "matter was of less importance than the form of the words that gave it utterance, that the setting of the ring was of more esteem than the diamond it displayed." Strong emotion and gushing passion were thought unbefitting. The deep feelings of the soul were not to be disturbed, and even "truth" was often "cut short to make a period round." Harmony of versification, melody of rhyme, trim and courtly diction, did duty for the nobler charms of poetry—true passion and imagination. It was an artificial age, and was strongly reflected by those who "held the mirror up to nature." Yet the nature they reflected was not genuine; it was that of the court and the drawing-room. But matters had come to a crisis. The public had grown tired of art and longed for a return to nature. One after another the poets were breaking loose from the bonds of fashion. The influence of the new school of poetic criticism, founded by the Wartons, and the publication of *Percy's Reliques*, were doubtless the two most potent agencies that contributed to the furtherance of the change, from the classical to the romantic spirit, which had already begun to manifest itself in the tastes of the people. The poets catching the breath of the true but forgotten inspiration of the past, while clinging to the polished form of the verse, gradually began to forsake the clear-cut, artificial spirit of the school of Pope, and seek for "subjects and forms of expression in a wider, more passionate and more natural sphere of nature and emotion."

It was during this period that Gray wrote—at the period when art had attained perfection, and when the public taste was calling for something more than art, when it was beginning to demand again the freshness, naturalness, and sprightly vivacity of the early poetry of the language. Accordingly, in his poetry are seen all the characteristics of this transition. There is in his versification all the polish of Pope. In fact, there is no more exquisitely elaborated and mechanically perfect poetry in the language. But with these is found also a spirit strongly antagonistic to that of this school. In the richness of his fancy, the rolling swell of his melodious verse, and the stately majesty of his tone, is perceptible a return to nature and her beauties. True, his verse is tinged with the didactic tendencies of the times, and attempts, in its somewhat gloomy grandeur, to pursue a moralizing strain ; yet there breathes throughout his poems, the reviving inspiration which culminated in the poetry of Cowper and Wordsworth.

The same remarks apply, in a slightly modified form, to Goldsmith. Writing at a somewhat later period than Gray, the gradual advance of poetic taste is clearly traceable in his utterances. Making all allowance for the different dispositions of the poets—the idle, inconstant, unstudious rambler, and the busy, persevering, toiling hermit—there is a laborious, unwearying labor in polishing and perfecting the versification, yet the polish is scarcely equal to that of Gray ; there is, too, an attempt, futile though it be, at theorizing in verse. But whilst he conforms thus far to the fashion of the times, he exhibits a studied avoidance of the antithetical contrasts, epigrammatic pointedness, and diamond-like hardness of the poets of the Augustan age of Queen Anne

During the period of transition, in which these two poets wrote, a copious supply of poetry was not wanting, yet scarcely anything that was then written can be said to have lived. From the death of Pope (1744) till the appearance of Cowper's poems, was one of the most barren periods in genuine and enduring poetical merit, in the whole course of our literature. Perhaps, the only poems of this time, which have survived until the present and possess any fair prospect of immortality, are those of Gray, Goldsmith, and Collins. It would, however, be a mistake to attribute the decay of poetry entirely to the dominant literary taste of the time; for, unfavorable as it undoubtedly was, to the production of poetry of the highest order, it will be found, that the moral and political tendencies of that age were still more effective in depressing poetical genius and in restraining the activity of the Muse.

England had been for many years sunk under the wave of Deism and religious indifference, which was partly the result of the French influence that followed the return of the exiled Stuart king, and partly arose as a natural reaction from the austerity of the Puritanical piety. The Protestant churches had lost much of their vitality and exercised but little influence over the masses. Owing to their poverty, ignorance, and great increase in numbers, the lower orders became in the large towns grossly degraded and brutal; and in the rural districts, being unprovided with moral or religious training of any kind, their condition was, if possible, still more deplorable. The higher circles, not to mention the prominent statesmen of the time, made a scoff at religion, and fully vindicated their contempt for all morality by the wickedness and open profligacy of their lives. "In the middle classes," says Greene, "the old piety lived on unchanged, and it was from this class that a religious revival burst forth at the close of Walpole's ministry, which changed in a few years the whole temper of English society." This great movement had, for some years, been producing its purifying effects upon English manners and English taste, when our poets appeared in succession upon the scene. The profligacy which had disgraced the upper classes, had now largely disappeared, and "the foulness which had infested literature ever since the Restoration," had been nearly banished from the land. Notwithstanding the improvement which had been effected, the prevailing spirit of the age was still unpoetic. Our greatest poets have arisen during periods of remarkable daring or of profound faith. Chaucer appeared in the age of the conquest of France; Shakespeare, when faith was attesting its sincerity at the stake. With the decay of the scepticism of Bolingbroke and Pope, society once more began to assume a phase, more sincere and, consequently, more conducive to the growth and development of the true spirit of poetry. Still the influence exerted by the public men of the day was little favorable to the cultivation of poetry.

In the reign of Charles the Second, Dorset had introduced a system of patronage, which for many years was extensively practised in England. At no period in English history, have literary men enjoyed so richly the assistance of those in power as during the reigns of William the Third, Anne, and George the First. Then almost every writer who could attract public attention, was immediately favored with a pension, a sinecure, or a commission. Rowe, Locke, Newton, Prior, Gay, and Steele were a few of the multitude who were placed above indigence by this system of princely patronage. But Harley and Bolingbroke were succeeded by Walpole. Walpole was a wise tactician.

but his tactics took no literary turn. The money which his predecessors had so nobly spent in fostering the literary talent of the country, he needed for purposes of corruption, and poets were left to starve, or beg, or "tear with wolfish teeth" their scanty morsel in some dark Grub-street cellar, for aught the administration cared. As it was a period of transition in the spirit of poetry, so was it also in the poet's audience and means of support. Government patronage had ceased, never again to revive except in fitful and uncertain flashes. The age of dedication, in which the poet, by feeding the vanity of the great, by

" Heaping the shrine of luxury and pride
With incense kindled at the Muse's flame,"

had managed to bring his works before the public, was "expiring through flattery." The Bookseller system, by which writers at first received a starving pittance from the publisher, was only just beginning, so that by this means the best writers of the day could barely secure a livelihood. The great world had not yet become the audience of the poet; and the bookseller's customers were consequently confined to the few. Such a period could not but be one of great privation and suffering to those who had "fallen upon these evil days." "Even an author," says Lord Macaulay, "whose reputation was established and whose works were popular, such an author as Thomson, whose *Seasons* were in every library, such an author as Fielding, whose *Pasquin* had had a greater run than any drama since the *Beggars' Opera*, was sometimes glad to obtain, by pawning his best coat, the means of dining on tripe at a cookshop underground, where he could wipe his hands, after his greasy meal, on the back of a Newfoundland dog." If there is any truth in what Dr. Cheyne of Bath told Thomson, "that as you put birds' eyes out to make them sing the sweeter, so you should keep poets poor to animate their genius," the latter were in a suitable condition for their labor.

A few, like Churchill, by making poetry a vehicle for political satire and party strife, had succeeded in gaining the ear of the cabinet, and consequently in receiving such material assistance as it was able to afford. But even this sort of patronage was hastening to an end, for it had been employed only for the support of party, and the right of the Press to discuss public affairs was no sooner established than "the hacks of Grub-street were superseded by publicists of a high moral temper and literary excellence; and philosophers like Coleridge or statesmen like Canning turned to influence public opinion through the columns of the Press." Thus poet and pamphleteer were abandoned to the neglect described by Crabbe in his *Newspaper:*

> "A daily swarm, that banish every Muse,
> Come flying forth, and mortals call them News:
> For these, unread, the noblest volumes lie;
> For these, in sheets, unsoiled, the Muses die."

From this brief survey of the literary, moral, and political phases of the period in which Gray and Goldsmith lived and wrote, the student will be able to form such an estimate of its leading characteristics, and to apprehend so much of its general features, as will assist him in understanding the relation in which these poets stand to the history and development of the poetical literature of the language, and in comprehending something of the condition of these poets, and of the more important opinions, tendencies, and influences which united to produce their poetical theory, and largely to determine the form and the spirit of their productions.

CHRONOLOGICAL PARALLEL.

A. D.	ENGLISH HISTORY AND LITERATURE.	LIFE OF GRAY.	LIFE OF GOLDSMITH.
1716	Garrick b. Septennial Bill.	Born December 26th.	
1718	Parnell d. Eusden, Poet Laureate.		
1719	Addison d.		
1720	South Sea Bubble.		
1721	Collins b. Robertson b. Walpole, premier.		
1722	Atterbury impeached. Jos. Warton b.		
1723	Adam Smith b.		
1724	*The Drapier Letters.*		
1725	Pope's *Homer's Odyssey.*		
1726	*Gulliver's Travels.* Thomson's *Winter.*		
1727	Accession of George II.		
1728	Percy b. Thos. Warton b. Pope's *Dunciad.*		Born November 10th.
1729	Congreve d. Steele d.		
1730	Colley Cibber, Poet Laureate. Burke b.		Family leave Pallas for Lissoy.
1731	Defoe d. Cowper b.		Sent to Miss Delap.
1732	Cumberland b. Gay d.		
1733	Pope's *Essay on Man* (2nd pt.). Excise Bill.		
1734		Goes to Cambridge.	Sent to school to Byrne.
1735	Beattie b. Pope's *Moral Essays.*		
1736	Porteous Riots.		To Rev. Mr. Griffin's.
1737	Gibbon b. Green d.		
1738	McPherson b. Johnson's *London.*	Leaves University.	
1739		Goes to the Continent.	To Rev. Mr. Campbell's.
1740	Sir Philip Francis b.		
1741	Richardson's *Pamela.*	Returns to England.	To Rev. Pat'k Hughes'.
1742	Walpole resigns.	Begins *Elegy.* Writes *Ode on Spring* and *Ode on Eton College.* Takes B.C.L.	
1743	Savage d. The Pelhams.		
1744	Pope d.		
1745	Swift d. Walpole d. The 'Forty-five.'		Enters Trinity College.
1746			
1747		Meets Mason. *Ode on Cat. Ode on Eton College.*	His father dies.

CHRONOLOGICAL PARALLEL.

A. D.	ENGLISH HISTORY AND LITERATURE.	LIFE OF GRAY.	LIFE OF GOLDSMITH.
1748	Thomson d. Peace of Aix-la-Chapelle.		
1749			Takes his B.A.
1750	Dr. Johnson's *Rambler*.	*Elegy* completed.	At home.
1751	Sheridan b. Bolingbroke d.	*Elegy* published.	
1752	Chatterton b. *Adventurer*.		Tutor at Mr. Flinn's. Starts out to study law. To Edinburgh to study medicine.
1753	The *World*.	*Long Story*.	
1754	Crabbe b. *Connoisseur*. Fielding d.		To Leyden. European Travels.
1755	Dr. Johnson's *Dictionary*.		
1756	Seven years' War begins.	Removes to Pembroke Hall.	Returns to England.
1757	Cibber d. Whitehead, Poet Laureate. Coalition of Newcastle and Pitt.	Offered the Laureateship. *Bard* and *Progress of Poesy*.	Teaches for Dr. Milner. Writes for *Monthly Review*.
1758	Dr. Johnson's *Idler*.		Fails at Examination.
1759	Burns b. Quebec taken.	At British Museum.	*Life of Voltaire. Inquiry. The Bee.* Writes for *British Magazine* and *Public Ledger*.
1760	*Poems of Ossian*. Accession of George III.		
1761	Richardson d.		*Citizen of the World*.
1762	Lord Bute, premier. *North Briton*.		*Life of Beau Nash*.
1763	Literary Club founded. Grenville Ministry.		
1764	Right of the Press to discuss public affairs first established.	Tour to Kent.	*History of England. Traveller.*
1765	Rockingham takes office. Young d. *Percy's Reliques*.	Tour to Scotland.	*Experimental Philosophy*.
1766	Mosaic Ministry.		*Vicar of Wakefield. Collection of Essays.*
1768	Sterne d. Grafton takes office.	Professor of History. *Fatal Sisters*.	*Good-Natured Man*.
1769	*Letters of Junius*.	*Installation Ode*. Tour to Cumberland.	M.B. at Oxford. *Roman History*.
1770	Lord North takes office. Wordsworth b. Chatterton d.		*Deserted Village. Life of Parnell. Life of Bolingbroke.*
1771	Walter Scott b.		*Haunch of Venison. English History*.
		Death, 30th July.	
1772	Coleridge b.		
1773			*She stoops to Conquer.*
1774	Southey b. Lord Clive d.		Death, 4th April; Burial, 9th April. *Retaliation. Animated Nature.*

LIFE OF GOLDSMITH.

When the assembled wits had decided to place the best epitaph upon Dryden's tomb that had ever been chiselled, Atterbury exclaimed, "'Dryden' is enough; they who know his works, want no more, they who do not know them, would not be enlightened by the most eloquent eulogy." True as these words are of Dryden, they are even more applicable to Goldsmith. As we read his works, his character gradually unfolds itself with each successive page, and we become familiar with the virtues, the weaknesses, and the foibles of our author. In one part or other of his writings, he has left us a complete autobiography of himself, drawn by a faithful, yet gentle hand. We smile and sympathize, or admire and love, as we meet, on every page, a genial, easy, and unceasing flow of good humor, good sense, and good feeling; as we see, in every character he has sketched, his own artless benevolence and fitfulness, his kindness and waywardness, or trace in their blunderings and buffetings, the mischances, ludicrous scenes, or laughable mistakes of his own life.

The Goldsmiths were a respectable, but unthrifty race, whose "hearts were in the right place, but whose heads seemed to be doing anything but what they ought." Accordingly the Rev. Charles Goldsmith, Oliver's father, married very young and very poor, and so was obliged for some years to "pray and starve" on forty pounds a year, in a small rural curacy at Pallas, a remote hamlet in the county of Longford, in Ireland. It was here that

Oliver, the second son of a family of four sons and two daughters, was born, on the 10th of November, 1728. While he was yet a child, his father was presented to the rectorship of Kilkenny West, in Westmeath, worth £200 a year. The family consequently exchanged the antique mansion and lonely wilds of Pallas for an elegant rectory situated on the busy high-road leading to Lissoy. Here, Oliver spent his boyhood days, and here, he received his early education. When only about three years old, he was sent to an old lady's private school to learn his letters. At the end of four years, she pronounced him a dunce, and passed him over to the hands of the village schoolmaster, Thomas (or, as the boys had it, Paddy) Byrne. Byrne, educated for a teacher, had enlisted in the army, served abroad in Queen Anne's time, and had risen to the rank of quarter-master. On his return from service, he had engaged to drill the urchins of Lissoy in reading, writing and arithmetic; but, like many a teacher whose knowledge is limited, yet whose tongue is facile, he gilded over his deficiencies by entertaining his wondering scholars with an exhaustless fund of stories. Instead of teaching them their lessons, he told them stories of ghosts and banshees, of robbers and pirates, of rapparees and smugglers, of the exploits of Peterborough and Stanhope, and of various incidents in which Thomas Byrne was the hero. Besides his facility in story-telling, he was an enthusiastic admirer of the ancient Irish bards whom he fancied he could imitate. Such a tutor was just the person to produce deep and lasting impressions on the imaginative mind of young Oliver who, before he was eight years of age, had begun to scribble verses of poetry. Some of these lines coming under the notice of his mother, she readily perceived that her son was a poetical genius, and from that time urged upon his father the necessity of giving the lad an education befitting his abilities. The expense of educating his eldest son, Henry, had so straitened the father's narrow income, that he had determined to put Oliver to a trade; but the mother's earnest solicitations won the day, and it was decided to give him a University education. Hence, on his recovery from a severe attack of small-pox, he was placed under the care of the Rev. Mr. Griffin, of Elphin. One evening while here, when a number of young people had assembled at his uncle's for a dance, the fiddler, turning Oliver's short clumsy figure and pock-marked face into ridicule, called him "Æsop." This was too much for his sensitive nature, and stopping short, he replied: "Heralds proclaim aloud this saying—See Æsop dancing and his monkey playing." This repartee raised him greatly in the estimation of his friends, several of whom—especially his uncle, the Rev. Thomas Contarine—contributed means to place him in a school possessing advantages superior to those afforded at Elphin. He was therefore removed to a school kept by the Rev. Mr. Campbell, at Athlone, and, after two years, transferred to one at Edgeworthstown, under the supervision of the Rev. Patrick Hughes. He does not appear to have been distinguished at any or these schools—except, indeed, by his easy, idle disposition, and blundering manners. No favorite with the teacher, he was the leader in the sports of the playground, and never hindmost in any schoolboy prank.

With this preparation, he was sent up to Trinity College, Dublin. He was now in his seventeenth year, eccentric, idle, and thoughtless. His sister having married a wealthy gentleman, named Hodson, her father deemed it a point of honor to furnish her with a suitable dowry, and, acting on this impulse, so embarrassed the family circumstances, that it was found impossible to give Oliver the same advantages as his brother, Henry. He accordingly entered College, as a sizar. The sizars paid nothing for tuition or board, and only a trifle for the rooms, but were required to perform various menial duties around the college. This, as might be expected, was very galling to the proud spirit of young Oliver; yet, while enduring these indignities, in order to enjoy the advantages of the institution, he neglected his studies, quarrelled with his tutor, received a public reprimand for joining in an attack on a bailiff, violated the college rules by giving a supper and dance to some of his city friends, won an exhibition of thirty shillings, and was turned to the foot for playing buffoon in his class.

While he was at Dublin his father died, leaving the family very poorly provided for, so that Oliver's situation became still more painful. To relieve his necessities he occasionally wrote songs, sold them for five shillings each, and then squandered the money. However, by the aid of his uncle, he was enabled to remain at college till he took his degree in 1749. He then returned home, spending three years, partly with his mother, who had taken a small cottage at Ballymahon, and partly with his brother-in-law, Hodson, at Lissoy. He was now twenty-one, and it became necessary to decide on some profession. His friends urged him to enter the church. After some difficulty his objections were withdrawn, and he began to qualify himself for Orders. The time for his ordination came. He presented himself to the bishop, dressed in scarlet breeches, and was, in consequence, rejected. He then became tutor in a wealthy family, but threw up the situation in a dispute over a game of cards. On receiving his wages he bought a fine horse, and set out for Cork, intending to sail for America; but after six weeks he returned home on a wretched nag and without a penny in his pocket. Next he determined to study law. His friends provided him with a purse of fifty pounds, with which he set out for London, but on his way he met an old acquaintance at Dublin, who took him to a gambling-house and stripped him of his money. At the suggestion of Dean Goldsmith of Cloyne, a distant relative, he then determined to study physic. His trusting friends again subscribed the funds, and he set out for Edinburgh, where he arrived in the autumn of 1752. Here he remained for eighteen months, studying, riding into the Highlands, gambling, singing Irish songs, or telling Irish stories. At the end of that time, he persuaded his good uncle, Contarine, to furnish him with funds to complete his medical studies at the University of Leyden. For Leyden he forthwith left Edinburgh. On arriving at this famous University, he recommenced his studies and his gambling. What progress he made in the former is uncertain, but, by the latter, he soon lost the last shilling of the £33, with which he had left Scotland. His friend, Ellis, lent him a few pounds with which to return to Paris, but he generously spent the whole, in purchasing some costly tulip roots for his affectionate uncle. Penniless and proud, he now determined to make a tour of the Continent on foot, and so with one spare shirt, a flute, and a guinea, he set out on his journey, visiting France, Germany, Switzerland, and Italy. In the story of the "Philosophic Vagabond," in the *Vicar of Wakefield*, he has given us some delightful reminiscences of his experiences in these wanderings,

"Remote, unfriended, melancholy, slow,"

in which he made those observations upon the peculiar characteristics of the various countries and their inhabitants, which he has, in his own easy, graceful style, recorded for the delight of all future ages, in the *Travel-*

ler. At Padua he remained for some months. Here, it is probable, his medical studies were resumed, and from this University, he tells us, he received his medical degree.

His generous uncle, whose slender remittances had never entirely ceased, died about this time, and the wanderer was compelled to seek his native shore. So after two years of roaming about on the Continent, he landed at Dover in 1756.

"Without friends, recommendation, money, or impudence," he arrived in London. Here, his flute had no attractions, nor could his philosophy supply his wants. He was compelled to seek other employment. He tried to turn his medical knowledge to advantage, but without avail. He then became strolling-player, but his face and figure soon drove him from the boards. Next, he is found pounding drugs in a chemist's laboratory near Fish Street. Through the friendship of Dr. Sleigh, an old fellow-student, he was enabled to commence the practice of physic in Bankside, Southwark, but his patients were chiefly among the poorest and humblest classes of society. To eke out the miserable pittance thus received, he began to do some hack-work for the booksellers. A few months later, and we find him usher in a school kept by Dr. Milner, at Peckham. His bitter experiences in this situation, he has left us in a lively sketch in the sixth number of the *Bee*, and in the history of "George Primrose." While thus employed, Mr. Griffiths, proprietor of the *Monthly Review*, being in need of increased writers in order to cope with the opposition which he now met from the *Critical Review* under the able conduct of Dr. Smollett, engaged Goldsmith for a year, at a small regular salary, with board and lodging. Irksome as the slavery of an usher had been, the vassalage of the bookseller and his critical wife was still more unbearable. At the end of five months, the engagement was broken off. After some further occasional and ill-paid contributions to various Reviews, he returned in deep want to Dr. Milner's, and took charge of the school during the Doctor's illness. He next received a medical appointment in the service of the East India Company. To raise money for the expected voyage, he set to work to write a treatise to be entitled *An Inquiry into the Present State of Polite Learning in Europe;* but before it was completed the appointment had been cancelled. He then presented himself for examination as hospital mate. The suit of clothes in which he appeared had been secured by writing four articles for Griffiths' *Monthly Review.* He failed at the examination, and pawned the unpaid-for clothes to relieve his landlady's distress. The *Life of Voltaire* was written at this time, to pacify the demand of Griffiths for the return of the suit of clothes and the books he had reviewed.

In 1759, appeared the *Inquiry,* a work of little value now-a-days, but which, to the grace and charm of its style, added much that then commanded public attention.

This was the age of periodicals, and Goldsmith must needs have his. The *Bee* first appeared on the 6th of October, 1759. It was to be issued every Saturday, and the price was threepence. It was filled with essays in great variety, penned in Goldsmith's neat and elegant style, but it failed to charm the public of the day; and its short career of eight weeks closed on the 29th of November. Whilst publishing the *Bee,* Goldsmith had been writing for other periodicals, the *Busy Body* and the *Critical Review.* He soon after became an important contributor to the *British Magazine* and to the *Public Ledger.* The series of letters which appeared in the *Ledger* was afterwards republished under the title of the

Citizen of the World. These letters, purporting to be addressed by a Chinese traveller to his friends at home, contain some lively and humorous sketches of English society, and have been "justly praised, for their fresh original perception, their delicate delineation of life and manners, their wit and humor, their playful and diverting satire, their exhilarating gaiety, and their clear and lively style."

Two other anonymous works were published about this time, *The Life of Beau Nash,* and *The History of England in a Series of Letters from a Nobleman to his Son.* The latter became exceedingly popular, and was attributed in turn to Lords Chesterfield, Orrery, and Lyttleton.

It was during these years that Goldsmith became acquainted with several of the distinguished literary characters of the time. Dr. Percy, renowned for his collection of English ballads, had some years before introduced himself to Goldsmith while the latter sat "writing his *Inquiry* in a wretched, dirty room in which there was but one chair, and when he, from civility, offered it to his visitor, was obliged himself to sit in the window." He managed to bring about a meeting between Goldsmith and the great literary autocrat of the period, Dr. Johnson. Among his acquaintances, also, were now the distinguished painters, Hogarth and Reynolds. At the house of Reynolds, he was introduced to more notable company than he had yet been accustomed to meet; and on the formation of the Literary Club in 1763, he was invited to become one of its members. This club which was suggested by Reynolds, originally consisted of Johnson, Burke, Beauclerc, Nugent, Bennet, Langton, Hawkins, Chamier, Reynolds, and Goldsmith. Its meetings were held once a week at the Turk's-head inn, in Gerrard-street, Soho, and its conversations exercised no little influence on the literature of the time. But though Goldsmith's circumstances were now greatly improved, life still seems to have been a struggle with him. Sometimes he revelled in plenty, but oftener was pining in want. One morning in the winter of 1764, he sent for Dr. Johnson, to come to him immediately, as he was in trouble. Johnson sent him a guinea, and as soon as he was dressed called to see him. He found that Goldsmith had changed the guinea, and procured a bottle of Madeira, over which he was disputing with his landlady who had that morning arrested him for arrears of rent. Johnson replaced the cork, and begged his friend to calm himself and consider how the money was to be obtained. The latter thereupon produced a novel upon which he had been engaged. After glancing over the manuscript, Johnson perceived that the work possessed rare merit, went out, sold it to a bookseller for £60, brought back the money, and the rent was paid. The novel which thus passed into the hands of the publisher, but which lay unprinted for upwards of two years, was the *Vicar of Wakefield*. Goldsmith was not yet known to the public as an author, and the bookseller had probably made his bargain depending largely on the judgment of Johnson. Soon all this was to be changed, for he was to have a reputation of his own, that would not only warrant the publication of the *Vicar*, but give his future productions a ready popularity.

In 1764, the *Traveller* was published, and Goldsmith was at once recognized as a poet of genuine worth. The ablest critics of the day joined in lauding the poem as worthy of a high place amongst our English classics, and Johnson, under whose fostering care it had been completed, introduced it to the public by a kindly notice in the *Critical Review*. The appearance of the *Traveller* was the great turning point in Goldsmith's career. It raised him in the estimation of the booksellers, opened his way into better society, and introduced him to the notice of the great. The Earl of Northumberland expressed a desire to serve him, but the generous-hearted poet recommended his brother Henry, saying of himself "that he looked to the booksellers for support, that they were his best friends, and that he was not inclined to forsake them for others."

He took advantage of his present popularity to collect and republish many of his essays which had appeared anonymously in various periodicals; and, that he might have some permanent means of support, again resumed the medical profession, hoping that he might now secure a higher class of patients; but meeting only disappointment, he soon abandoned it in disgust, to return to the service of his old "patrons."

The fourth edition of the *Traveller* had just been issued, and Goldsmith was enjoying the reputation of being the first poet of his age, when the *Vicar of Wakefield* was published. This charming novel of English domestic life, the earliest of its kind, was at first but coldly received by the Club, the leading journals of the day, and the higher classes of society. Yet, surely, if slowly, it grew in favor. Three editions were printed within four months, and the author lived to see it translated into several continental languages. Its plot is confused, and many of the incidents are highly improbable, but its quiet humor and lively wit amuse us at every turn and sparkle on every page. It overflows with a kindly sympathy for the failings of the race; and the characters are drawn with such truth to nature, that they cannot fail to reach the heart. Its moral, too, is excellent—to show us how our lives may be made happy by "patience in suffering, persevering reliance on the providence of God, quiet labor, and an indulgent forgiveness of the faults of others." Little wonder that such a book has passed from country to country, and obtained a wider popularity than any other of its kind.

The celebrity which Goldsmith won by the publication of the *Traveller* and *Vicar* materially raised his social standing, but did not equally improve his circumstances. Debts and drudgery were still his portion. He was compelled to toil for the booksellers as before, with this difference, that his services now received a better remuneration. In the midst of this thankless labor, his leisure was devoted to work of another kind. He had won laurels as a poet, and as a novelist: now he was emboldened to try his fortune as a writer of comedy. His first attempt, the *Good-Natured Man*, was acted at Covent Garden in 1768. It had been finished early in the preceding year, but, though recommended by Johnson, Burke, and Reynolds, he had much difficulty in inducing the managers to accept it. Its reception at a time when sentimentalism was the rage, could not be hearty; yet the author received from his benefit nights and from the sale of the copyright upwards of £500, a sum many times larger than he had received for any of his previous writings. The plot of the *Good-Natured Man*, like all Goldsmith's plots, is very imperfect, but in character, repartee, and humor, this comedy has few superiors. Yet at the time when it was brought on the stage its very excellencies were its ruin. Anything that moved the audience to laughter was sure to be "hissed" from pit to boxes; and accordingly the very scene which Goldsmith considered the best—and posterity has endorsed his opinion—was received with marked disapprobation, and had to be withdrawn after the first night.

With so great a sum as £500 in his possession, and with no small reputation as a poet, novelist, and dramatic author, Goldsmith thought proper to remove into more commodious and respectable lodgings. Leaving his shabby rooms at Jeffs', he leased apartments in Brick Court, Middle Temple, which he proceeded to furnish in elegant style, and then began a course of life which burdened him with debts and mental distress for the rest of his days. His pen was now more actively engaged than ever in writing for the booksellers, and his fame commanded a high return for his labor. For Tom Davies he compiled a *History of Rome* for which he received £300. Its rapid sale prompted Davies to offer £500 for a *History of England*, and at the same time Goldsmith was at work upon his *Animated Nature* for which Griffin agreed to give him 800 guineas.

These works are all written with the author's own easy, graceful flow of narrative, and never fail to please and interest the reader ; but the facts are taken at secondhand, without any elaborate inquiry into their correctness; and consequently he has been led into making some ludicrous errors and absurd statements. Yet Johnson ranked him, as an historian, above Robertson, and declared that he would make his *Animated Nature* as "entertaining as a Persian tale." His histories, inaccurate as they are, have done much to make their subject interesting to young people, and they still rank amongst the most popular of abridged works.

While busy upon these toilsome tasks, he found a few spare moments left him to cultivate the muse, and added much to his poetical fame by publishing, in 1770, the *Deserted Village*. This poem leaped at once to the height of popularity, no fewer than five editions being required within the first three months. Nor was its popularity ephemeral, for the judgment of the time has been endorsed by tens of thousands of readers since, and seems likely never to be reversed. Its reasoning may be erroneous, its proposed theory, unestablished; it may be pervaded by the "unpardonable fault" pointed out by Macaulay, yet, like its author whose errors we regret, that we may the better remember his kindly heart and deep human sympathy, its lovely description, its touching complaints, its sweet images, steal away our heart, while its "unity, completeness, polish, and perfectness" take captive our judgment. Like the poems of the time, it has a didactic purpose in view. But it is not its theory that pleases us. We do not stop to inquire whether the "peasantry" were really being decimated, or whether

"'Trade's proud empire hastes to swift decay ;"

it is the genuine sympathy of the poet for the destruction of the scenes of his youth, the warm and penetrating sorrow which he expresses for the race who, he supposes, is being cruelly driven from its native soil, that so touchingly impress us.

But the "draggle-tailed muses," as Goldsmith was once heard to say, furnished but a scanty means of subsistence. Such at least did they in his case. His poetical fame brought him directly but small returns. Hence we find him, soon after the publication of the *Deserted Village*, again at work for his old "patrons," the booksellers. He made an abridgment of his Roman History, wrote an inferior *Life of Parnell*, and compiled a *Life of Lora Bolingbroke*. The biography of Bolingbroke, though written at a time of great political excitement, is entirely free from party prejudice, and gives a clear, entertaining account of this great statesman's life. In 1773, Goldsmith with great difficulty, induced the managers to allow him to try his chances, a second time, with a comedy entitled *She Stoops to Conquer*. This play, like its predecessor, the *Good-Natured Man*, was based upon character and humor. The public taste still demanded the sentimental comedy of Cumberland and Kelly, and scouted everything that tended to produce boisterous mirth. The fun of Goldsmith's first comedy had driven it from the boards, and the fun of this one was uproarious when compared with it. It was brought out by Coleman, at Covent Garden. The actors, as well as the managers, are said to have had little hopes of its success. But all were disappointed, when pit, and galleries, and boxes, rang with peal upon peal of uncontrollable laughter. The play ran on every night for the remainder of the season, and is one of the very few comedies of the time which still retain possession of the stage. But Goldsmith's receipts from the success of the *Good-Natured Man* were not paid in fame alone, for he reaped a rich pecuniary harvest. Yet all the money he received, and all he could manage to raise on works to be written, but not yet begun, were insufficient to satisfy the demands of his creditors, or to brighten his prospects for the future.

We find him trying to forget his troubles by a visit to the country, by attendance at the Club, and by frequenting gay society. But it was all in vain. His unfinished but prepaid engagements became doubly burdensome, as presenting no means of relief. Though his "knack at hoping" seemed to be failing him, yet he was full of plans, and at times was hard at work. He had almost completed his *Animated Nature* and *Grecian History*; was preparing a third edition of his *History of England*, revising his *Inquiry*, translating Scarron's *Comic Romance*, and arranging his papers for the most extensive work he had ever yet contemplated—*A Popular Dictionary of*

Arts and Sciences. His plans for this *Dictionary*, though cheerfully entertained by his friends, did not secure the confidence of the booksellers, and the work was never completed.

In the midst of his disappointments and despondency, his poetical genius once more flashed forth in a little poem which he composed in reply to some gibing epitaphs written by his friends, while awaiting his usual late arrival at a dinner. Being unable to reply at the time he took to his pen, and with a few inimitable strokes sketched, in clear and vigorous language, the character of some nine or ten of his most intimate friends. He gave it the title of *Retaliation*, but, like his own generous nature, it had in it too much of the "milk of human kindness" to contain revenge. Short and unfinished as it is, its good sense and humorous raillery, its exquisite discrimination and graphic truth, will always mark it as a masterpiece.

But this facile pen must write no more. An illness, if not induced, at least aggravated, by his pressing necessities and deranged circumstances, seized him while laboring under his present depression. He complained of pain in his head, and of fever. Contrary to the advice of his medical attendants, he persisted in taking some powders from which he had formerly obtained relief in other disorders. His malady fluctuated for some days, and hopes were even entertained of his recovery; but his sleep left him, his mind was ill at ease, and his appetite was gone. At length he fell into a deep sleep from which he awoke in strong convulsions, which continued till death brought release on the 4th of April, 1774. He was in his forty-sixth year. His death produced a deep sensation among his friends. On hearing he was dead, Burke burst into tears, and Reynolds laid up his pencil for the remainder of the day. A public funeral and a tomb in Westminster were at first proposed, but subsequently given up, and he was privately interred in the burying ground of the Temple Church. Shortly after his death, a cenotaph was erected to his memory in Westminster Abbey. Nollekens was the sculptor, and the inscription was written by Dr. Johnson.

Of all our English writers there is none over whose memory the reader lingers with more affectionate remembrance than over that of Goldsmith. Not that his character was faultless; far from it. There is much to admire, but also much to regret. He was a compound of weakness and strength, and his life was full of inconsistencies. His head was ever devising plans which he lacked resolution and energy to carry out. Indolence and procrastination were part of his very nature. At school his lessons were neglected for some idle sport. At college he feasted his city friends, and graduated last on the list of Sizars. Of these habits the booksellers had always to complain; and for this reason they rejected the scheme of his proposed *Dictionary*. Few men were more ambitious than he, and his ambition led him at times to put forth great, if spasmodic, efforts to win the praise which he heard bestowed upon others. He strove to outshine Johnson in conversation, but his attempts brought upon him the derision of the Club. His vanity led him into exhibitions of jealousy, and even of envy. His extreme sensibility made him writhe under the jests of which he was made the object, but his forgiving nature could never avenge the insults heaped upon him. It need not for a moment be supposed that Goldsmith had more of envy, jealousy, and vanity than many of his associates, but his blundering, outspoken, and transparent nature made his failings more conspicuous. He was frivolous, improvident, profuse and sensual. His benevolence often outran his judgment, for the softness of his heart could hear no tale of distress without attempting whatever assistance lay in his power to relieve it.

Though he had graduated at Trinity College, and had professedly studied for the church and the medical profession, yet there was not a single subject of which he could be said to be master. He knew nothing thoroughly. His prose writings exhibit no evidences of depth or close examination, but are superficial and inaccurate. But whatever he knew he could tell with clearness, and surround with charming interest. When he looks within his own heart and gives utterance to the feelings which fill his breast, he expresses himself with a naturalness, a grace, and a tenderness, which bespeak the true poet and the man of broad and deep human sympathy. But when he goes beyond his own experiences, he always blunders, always fails. Happily, he has generally confined himself to subjects in which his acute and varied observation gave him a power that has largely compensated for his lack of imagination. His style is the perfection of ease. There is no straining after effect, no ponderous phrases, no heavily-turned periods. His words are aptly chosen, his diction select and terse, his language felicitous, and his taste excellent. Dealing chiefly with familiar topics, he always keeps above vulgarity, but he is at times justly chargeable with carelessness and want of precision in the construction of his sentences. In palliation of this, it may be said, that many of his productions were completed in great haste, under pressing necessities, and are not therefore fairly open to criticism. In everything he has written, there is an easy grace and elegance which have always made his writings popular, and which bid fair to perpetuate his fame as long as our language endures.

THE TRAVELLER;
OR A PROSPECT OF SOCIETY.

INTRODUCTION.

ALTHOUGH conjecture is the only guide as to the precise character of the earliest sketch of this poem, yet it is known, that it was first begun during Goldsmith's solitary wanderings in Switzerland about the year 1755, and sent home to his brother Henry, at that time a curate at Lissoy. The poet had kept it by him for several years, touching and retouching it. At last he ventured to shew it to Dr. Johnson who was so much pleased with it that he assisted in its completion, encouraged its publication, and, on its appearance, called public attention to it by an article in which he declared it would be difficult to find anything equal to it since the death of Pope—a period of about 20 years. It was published on the 19th of December 1764, but bears date 1765. Printed in quarto, and sold at one shilling and sixpence, it was the first of Goldsmith's works to which he had prefixed his name. Newberry was the publisher; and from him the poet received twenty guineas for the manuscript. Overlooking the great men, whose favor it might have given fortune to court by a dedication, the poet from the midst of his poverty dedicated the poem, with genuine affection, to his brother Henry. But, though the author took every precaution, that he might bury his production in obscurity, neither devoting it to political warfare, nor seeking the patronage of the great, yet he was unsuccessful; for, though it did not become instantaneously popular, it won favor so rapidly, that a second edition was called for in a month, soon after a third, then a fourth was issued, and finally the ninth appeared in the year the poet died. In these editions various alterations were made. Thirty-six new lines were added, and fourteen of the old ones were cancelled; "but," says Forster, "no honest thought disappeared, no manly word for the oppressed. The 'wanton judge' and his 'penal statutes' remained. But words quietly vanished here and there, that had spoken too plainly of the sordid past; and no longer did the poet proclaim, in speaking of the great, that, 'inly satisfied above their pomps he held his ragged pride.'" Of its plan, Lord Macaulay has well said: "No philosophical poem, ancient or modern, has a plan so noble, and at the same time so simple. An English wanderer, seated on a crag among the Alps, near the point where three great countries meet, looks down on the boundless prospect, reviews his long pilgrimage, recalls the varieties of scenery, of government, of religion, of national character which he has observed, and comes to the conclusion, just or unjust, that our happiness depends little on political institutions, and much on the temper of our own minds." The opinion, that the form of government exercises little or no influence on the happiness of the individual, was a favorite one with Dr. Johnson. Whether the poet has been successful in establishing this theory, or not, is so obvious that it seems needless to discuss the question. No amount of reasoning could ever make it appear that the happiness of the individual is not largely affected by the character of the government under which he lives— that the tyranny of the despot is as beneficial as the tempered sway of the constitutional sovereign. As no human contrivance is perfect, there are doubtless evils which no government can remove, and even hardships which it itself inflicts. One system of government may be better suited to one people than another ; and the form of government best adapted to the wants of a country depends on the characteristics of its inhabitants, and their advancement in civilization ; but it is vain to affirm that all kinds of government are equally effectual in securing the happiness of the people. If, however, this poem be closely examined, it will be found, that the conclusion, drawn in the closing lines which were partially supplied by Dr. Johnson, is very far from being the main theory which is attempted to be established in the body of the poem. The poet tells us at the outset that his design is to show, that by a natural compensation, people may be equally happy in every country, that of the "blessings which they share . . wisdom shall find an equal portion dealt to all mankind," and that the inhabitants of each country have their favorite method of attaining to happiness ; the Italians, by sensuality; the French, by gaiety ; the Swiss, by patriotism ; the Hollanders, by industry ; and the English, by liberty. But let it be carefully observed, that it is not the government of the country that is credited with affecting the happiness of the people—no mention of its effects being made until the poet comes to speak of England. We are inclined to the opinion that the allusion to the injurious effects of English freedom was suggested by the political turmoil of the time, after the poem was nearly completed, and that the conclusion, that governments can affect but little the happiness of the people, was an after-thought prompted by Dr. Johnson, or introduced in deference to his political paradox. After all, it is not the philosophical part of the poem that pleases. The reader is little careful to inquire what its theories are, or whether they are true or false. What delights us is not the creeds or doctrines it teaches. The happy descriptions of the different countries, their scenery, their climate, their productions, their inhabitants; all these, the poet has invested with a charm which makes even the peasant's 'shed' and his 'gestic lore' matters of lively interest. These pictures, he has skilfully placed side by side for the sake of contrast; Italy with all the profusion of her natural productions, and her weak, idle, and vicious races, is immediately followed by Switzerland with her sturdy, active, patriotic citizens; France with her gay, frivolous, honor-loving people, brings into stronger light Holland with her dull, plodding, money-loving natives; while the 'Britons' are added as an offset to all, exhibiting man in his noblest form—the 'lords of human kind.' Besides the skill with which the subject is handled, the poem is replete with noble sentiments. "It is built upon nature and rests on honest truth." Its language is plain, but forcible; condensed, but clear and familiar. The great care and skill with which its verse is elaborated, remind us of the neat and accurate versification of Pope. But if he imitated the poet of Twickenham in the form and polish of his numbers, it was only in these particulars. Though Goldsmith, influenced by the spirit of the age, tries to write an essay in poetry, yet his success is insured in proportion as he fails to reason. Simple and unadorned, his style has a naturalness and an ease that never fail to charm. If he has come short of establishing the theories proposed, he has, as Dr. Waller observes, "inculcated two great moralities in this poem: one, a deep moral feeling,—a home-love, the very soul of all patriotism; the other, a high moral principle of universal truth and application,—that man finds his greatest happiness in his own mind."

THE TRAVELLER.

DEDICATION.

TO THE REV. HENRY GOLDSMITH.

DEAR SIR,

I am sensible that the friendship between us can acquire no new force from the ceremonies of a dedication; and perhaps it demands an excuse thus to prefix your name to my attempts, which you decline giving with your own. But as a part of this poem was formerly written to you from Switzerland, the whole can now, with propriety, be only inscribed to you. It will also throw a light upon many parts of it, when the reader understands that it is addressed to a man, who, despising fame and fortune, has retired early to happiness and obscurity, with an income of forty pounds a year.

I now perceive, my dear brother, the wisdom of your humble choice. You have entered upon a sacred office, where the harvest is great and the laborers are but few; while you have left the field of ambition, where the laborers are many, and the harvest not worth carrying away. But of all kinds of ambition, what from the refinement of the times, from different systems of criticism, and from the divisions of party, that which pursues poetical fame is the wildest.

Poetry makes a principal amusement among unpolished nations; but in a country verging to the extremes of refinement, painting and music come in for a share. As these offer the feeble mind a less laborious entertainment, they at first rival poetry, and at length supplant her: they engross all that favor once shown to her, and, though but younger sisters, seize upon the elder's birthright.

DEDICATION.

Yet, however this art may be neglected by the powerful, it is still in great danger from the mistaken efforts of the learned to improve it. What criticisms have we not heard of late in favor of blank verse and Pindaric odes, choruses, anapests and iambics, alliterative care and happy negligence! Every absurdity has now a champion to defend it; and as he is generally much in the wrong, so he has always much to say; for error is ever talkative.

But there is an enemy to this art still more dangerous: I mean party. Party entirely distorts the judgment, and destroys the taste. When the mind is once infected with this disease, it can only find pleasure in what contributes to increase the distemper. Like the tiger, that seldom desists from pursuing man, after having once preyed upon human flesh, the reader, who has once gratified his appetite with calumny, makes ever after the most agreeable feast upon murdered reputation. Such readers generally admire some half-witted thing, who wants to be thought a bold man, having lost the character of a wise one. Him they dignify with the name of poet: his tawdry lampoons are called satires; his turbulence is said to be force, and his frenzy fire.

What reception a poem may find, which has neither abuse, party, nor blank verse to support it, I cannot tell, nor am I solicitous to know. My aims are right. Without espousing the cause of any party, I have attempted to moderate the rage of all. I have endeavored to show that there may be equal happiness in states that are differently governed from our own; that each state has a particular principle of happiness; and that this principle in each may be carried to a mischievous excess. There are few can judge better than yourself, how far these positions are illustrated in this poem. I am,

Dear Sir,

Your most affectionate brother,

OLIVER GOLDSMITH.

THE TRAVELLER;

OR

A PROSPECT OF SOCIETY.

   REMOTE, unfriended, melancholy, slow,
Or by the lazy Scheldt or wandering Po;
Or onward, where the rude Carinthian boor
Against the houseless stranger shuts the door;
Or where Campania's plain forsaken lies   5
A weary waste expanding to the skies;
Where'er I roam, whatever realms to see,
My heart untravelled fondly turns to thee:
Still to my Brother turns, with ceaseless pain,
And drags at each remove a lengthening chain.   10

   Eternal blessings crown my earliest friend,
And round his dwelling guardian saints attend;
Blest be that spot, where cheerful guests retire
To pause from toil, and trim their evening fire;
Blest that abode, where want and pain repair,   15
And every stranger finds a ready chair;
Blest be those feasts with simple plenty crowned,
Where all the ruddy family around
Laugh at the jests or pranks that never fail,
Or sigh with pity at some mournful tale,   20

Or press the bashful stranger to his food,
And learn the luxury of doing good.

But me, not destined such delights to share,
My prime of life in wandering spent and care;
Impelled, with steps unceasing, to pursue 25
Some fleeting good that mocks me with the view,
That, like the circle bounding earth and skies,
Allures from far, yet, as I follow, flies;
My fortune leads to traverse realms alone,
And find no spot of all the world my own. 30

E'en now, where Alpine solitudes ascend,
I sit me down a pensive hour to spend;
And, placed on high above the storm's career,
Look downward where an hundred realms appear;
Lakes, forests, cities, plains extending wide, 35
The pomp of kings, the shepherd's humbler pride.

When thus Creation's charms around combine,
Amidst the store, should thankless pride repine?
Say, should the philosophic mind disdain
That good which makes each humbler bosom vain? 40
Let school-taught pride dissemble all it can,
These little things are great to little man;
And wiser he whose sympathetic mind
Exults in all the good of all mankind.
Ye glittering towns, with wealth and splendor crowned; 45
Ye fields, where summer spreads profusion round;

Ye lakes, whose vessels catch the busy gale;
Ye bending swains, that dress the flowery vale;
For me your tributary stores combine:
Creation's heir, the world, the world is mine!　　　50

As some lone miser, visiting his store,
Bends at his treasure, counts, recounts it o'er;
Hoards after hoards his rising raptures fill,
Yet still he sighs, for hoards are wanting still:
Thus to my breast alternate passions rise,　　　55
Pleased with each good that Heaven to man supplies:
Yet oft a sigh prevails, and sorrows fall,
To see the hoard of human bliss so small;
And oft I wish, amidst the scene, to find
Some spot to real happiness consigned,　　　60
Where my worn soul, each wandering hope at rest,
May gather bliss to see my fellows blest.

But where to find that happiest spot below,
Who can direct, when all pretend to know?
The shuddering tenant of the frigid zone　　　65
Boldly proclaims that happiest spot his own;
Extols the treasures of his stormy seas,
And his long nights of revelry and ease:
The naked negro, panting at the line,
Boasts of his golden sands and palmy wine,　　　70
Basks in the glare, or stems the tepid wave,
And thanks his gods for all the good they gave.

Such is the patriot's boast, where'er we roam;
His first, best country ever is at home.
And yet, perhaps, if countries we compare,   75
And estimate the blessings which they share,
Though patriots flatter, still shall wisdom find
An equal portion dealt to all mankind;
As different good, by art or nature given,
To different nations makes their blessings even.   80

 Nature, a mother kind alike to all,
Still grants her bliss at labor's earnest call:
With food as well the peasant is supplied
On Idra's cliffs as Arno's shelvy side;
And though the rocky crested summits frown,   85
These rocks, by custom, turn to beds of down.
From art more various are the blessings sent;
Wealth, commerce, honor, liberty, content.
Yet these each other's power so strong contest,
That either seems destructive of the rest.   90
Where wealth and freedom reign, contentment fails,
And honor sinks where commerce long prevails.
Hence every state, to one loved blessing prone,
Conforms and models life to that alone.
Each to the favorite happiness attends,   95
And spurns the plan that aims at other ends;
Till, carried to excess in each domain,
This favorite good begets peculiar pain.

 But let us try these truths with closer eyes,
And trace them through the prospect as it lies: 100

Here for a while my proper cares resigned,
Here let me sit in sorrow for mankind ;
Like yon neglected shrub at random cast,
That shades the steep, and sighs at every blast.

Far to the right, where Apennine ascends, 105
Bright as the summer, Italy extends ;
Its uplands sloping deck the mountain's side,
Woods over woods in gay theatric pride ;
While oft some temple's mouldering tops between
With venerable grandeur mark the scene. 110

Could Nature's bounty satisfy the breast,
The sons of Italy were surely blest.
Whatever fruits in different climes were found,
That proudly rise, or humbly court the ground ;
Whatever blooms in torrid tracts appear, 115
Whose bright succession decks the varied year ;
Whatever sweets salute the northern sky
With vernal lives that blossom but to die ;
These here disporting own the kindred soil,
Nor ask luxuriance from the planter's toil ; 120
While sea-born gales their gelid wings expand
To winnow fragrance round the smiling land.

But small the bliss that sense alone bestows,
And sensual bliss is all the nation knows.
In florid beauty groves and fields appear, 125
Man seems the only growth that dwindles here.

Contrasted faults through all his manners reign :
Though poor, luxurious ; though submissive, vain ;
Though grave, yet trifling ; zealous, yet untrue ;
And even in penance planning sins anew. 130
All evils here contaminate the mind,
That opulence departed leaves behind ;
For wealth was theirs, not far removed the date,
When commerce proudly flourished through the state ;
At her command the palace learnt to rise, 135
Again the long-fallen column sought the skies,
The canvas glowed beyond e'en nature warm,
The pregnant quarry teemed with human form ;
Till, more unsteady than the southern gale,
Commerce on other shores displayed her sail ; 140
While nought remained of all that riches gave,
But towns unmanned and lords without a slave :
And late the nation found with fruitless skill
Its former strength was but plethoric ill.

Yet still the loss of wealth is here supplied 145
By arts, the splendid wrecks of former pride ;
From these the feeble heart and long-fallen mind
An easy compensation seem to find.
Here may be seen, in bloodless pomp arrayed,
The pasteboard triumph and the cavalcade, 150
Processions formed for piety and love,
A mistress or a saint in every grove.
By sports like these are all their cares beguiled ;
The sports of children satisfy the child.

Each nobler aim, represt by long control, 155
Now sinks at last, or feebly mans the soul;
While low delights, succeeding fast behind,
In happier meanness occupy the mind:
As in those domes, where Cæsars once bore sway,
Defaced by time and tottering in decay, 160
There in the ruin, heedless of the dead,
The shelter-seeking peasant builds his shed,
And, wondering man could want the larger pile,
Exults, and owns his cottage with a smile.

My soul, turn from them, turn we to survey 165
Where rougher climes a nobler race display,
Where the bleak Swiss their stormy mansion tread,
And force a churlish soil for scanty bread.
No product here the barren hills afford,
But man and steel, the soldier and his sword; 170
No vernal blooms their torpid rocks array,
But winter lingering chills the lap of May;
No zephyr fondly sues the mountain's breast,
But meteors glare, and stormy glooms invest.

Yet still, even here, content can spread a charm, 175
Redress the clime, and all its rage disarm.
Though poor the peasant's hut, his feast though small,
He sees his little lot the lot of all;
Sees no contiguous palace rear its head
To shame the meanness of his humble shed; 180

No costly lord the sumptuous banquet deal,
To make him loathe his vegetable meal;
But calm, and bred in ignorance and toil,
Each wish contracting, fits him to the soil.
Cheerful at morn, he wakes from short repose, 185
Breasts the keen air, and carols as he goes;
With patient angle trolls the finny deep,
Or drives his venturous ploughshare to the steep;
Or seeks the den where snow-tracks mark the way,
And drags the struggling savage into day. 190
At night returning, every labor sped,
He sits him down the monarch of a shed;
Smiles by his cheerful fire, and round surveys
His children's looks, that brighten at the blaze;
While his loved partner, boastful of her hoard, 195
Displays her cleanly platter on the board:
And haply too some pilgrim, thither led,
With many a tale repays the nightly bed.

Thus every good his native wilds impart,
Imprints the patriot passion on his heart; 200
And e'en those ills that round his mansion rise
Enhance the bliss his scanty fund supplies.
Dear is that shed to which his soul conforms,
And dear that hill which lifts him to the storms;
And as a child, when scaring sounds molest, 205
Clings close and closer to the mother's breast,
So the loud torrent and the whirlwind's roar
But bind him to his native mountains more.

Such are the charms to barren states assigned;
Their wants but few, their wishes all confined. 210
Yet let them only share the praises due;
If few their wants, their pleasures are but few;
For every want that stimulates the breast
Becomes a source of pleasure when redrest.
Whence from such lands each pleasing science flies, 215
That first excites desire, and then supplies;
Unknown to them, when sensual pleasures cloy,
To fill the languid pause with finer joy;
Unknown those powers that raise the soul to flame,
Catch every nerve, and vibrate through the frame. 220
Their level life is but a smouldering fire,
Unquenched by want, unfanned by strong desire;
Unfit for raptures, or, if raptures cheer
On some high festival of once a year,
In wild excess the vulgar breast takes fire, 225
Till, buried in debauch, the bliss expire.

But not their joys alone thus coarsely flow:
Their morals, like their pleasures, are but low;
For, as refinement stops, from sire to son,
Unaltered, unimproved, the manners run; 230
And love's and friendship's finely-pointed dart
Fall blunted from each indurated heart.
Some sterner virtues o'er the mountain's breast
May sit, like falcons cowering on the nest;
But all the gentler morals, such as play 235
Through life's more cultured walks, and charm the way,

These, far dispersed, on timorous pinions fly,
To sport and flutter in a kinder sky.

To kinder skies, where gentler manners reign,
I turn ; and France displays her bright domain. 240
Gay, sprightly land of mirth and social ease,
Pleased with thyself, whom all the world can please,
How often have I led thy sportive choir,
With tuneless pipe, beside the murmuring Loire,
Where shading elms along the margin grew, 245
And, freshened from the wave, the zephyr flew !
And haply, though my harsh touch, faltering still,
But mocked all tune, and marred the dancer's skill,
Yet would the village praise my wondrous power,
And dance, forgetful of the noontide hour. 250
Alike all ages. Dames of ancient days
Have led their children through the mirthful maze,
And the gay grandsire, skilled in gestic lore,
Has frisked beneath the burthen of threescore.

So blest a life these thoughtless realms display, 255
Thus idly busy rolls their world away :
Theirs are those arts that mind to mind endear,
For honor forms the social temper here :
Honor, that praise which real merit gains,
Or even imaginary worth obtains, 260
Here passes current ; paid from hand to hand,
It shifts in splendid traffic round the land :

From courts to camps, to cottages it strays,
And all are taught an avarice of praise.
They please, are pleased ; they give to get esteem, 265
Till, seeming blest, they grow to what they seem.

But while this softer art their bliss supplies,
It gives their follies also room to rise ;
For praise too dearly loved, or warmly sought,
Enfeebles all internal strength of thought ; 270
And the weak soul, within itself unblest,
Leans for all pleasure on another's breast.
Hence ostentation here, with tawdry art,
Pants for the vulgar praise which fools impart ;
Here vanity assumes her pert grimace, 275
And trims her robes of frieze with copper lace ;
Here beggar pride defrauds her daily cheer,
To boast one splendid banquet once a year :
The mind still turns where shifting fashion draws,
Nor weighs the solid worth of self-applause. 280

To men of other minds my fancy flies,
Embosomed in the deep where Holland lies.
Methinks her patient sons before me stand,
Where the broad ocean leans against the land,
And, sedulous to stop the coming tide, 285
Lift the tall rampire's artificial pride.
Onward, methinks, and diligently slow,
The firm connected bulwark seems to grow,

Spreads its long arms amidst the watery roar,
Scoops out an empire, and usurps the shore; 290
While the pent ocean, rising o'er the pile,
Sees an amphibious world beneath him smile ;
The slow canal, the yellow-blossomed vale,
The willow-tufted bank, the gliding sail,
The crowded mart, the cultivated plain; 295
A new creation rescued from his reign.

   Thus, while around the wave-subjected soil
Impels the native to repeated toil,
Industrious habits in each bosom reign,
And industry begets a love of gain. 300
Hence all the good from opulence that springs,
With all those ills superfluous treasure brings,
Are here displayed. Their much-loved wealth imparts
Convenience, plenty, elegance, and arts ;
But view them closer, craft and fraud appear, 305
Even liberty itself is bartered here.
At gold's superior charms all freedom flies ;
The needy sell it, and the rich man buys :
A land of tyrants, and a den of slaves,
Here wretches seek dishonorable graves, 310
And calmly bent, to servitude conform,
Dull as their lakes that slumber in the storm.

   Heavens ! how unlike their Belgic sires of old—
Rough, poor, content, ungovernably bold,
War in each breast, and freedom on each brow ; 315
How much unlike the sons of Britain now !

Fired at the sound, my genius spreads her wing,
And flies where Britain courts the western spring;
Where lawns extend that scorn Arcadian pride,
And brighter streams than famed Hydaspes glide. 320
There all around the gentlest breezes stray,
There gentle music melts on every spray;
Creation's mildest charms are there combined,
Extremes are only in the master's mind.
Stern o'er each bosom Reason holds her state, 325
With daring aims irregularly great;
Pride in their port, defiance in their eye,
I see the lords of human kind pass by;
Intent on high designs, a thoughtful band,
By forms unfashioned, fresh from Nature's hand, 330
Fierce in their native hardiness of soul,
True to imagined right, above control;
While even the peasant boasts these rights to scan,
And learns to venerate himself as man.

Thine, Freedom, thine the blessings pictured here, 335
Thine are those charms that dazzle and endear;
Too blest, indeed, were such without alloy,
But fostered even by freedom, ills annoy.
That independence Britons prize too high,
Keeps man from man, and breaks the social tie; 340
The self-dependent lordlings stand alone,
All claims that bind and sweeten life unknown:
Here by the bonds of nature feebly held,
Minds combat minds, repelling and repelled;

Ferments arise, imprisoned factions roar, 345
Represt ambition struggles round her shore,
Till, over-wrought, the general system feels
Its motions stop, or frenzy fire the wheels.

Nor this the worst. As nature's ties decay,
As duty, love, and honor fail to sway, 350
Fictitious bonds, the bonds of wealth and law,
Still gather strength, and force unwilling awe.
Hence all obedience bows to these alone,
And talent sinks, and merit weeps unknown;
Till time may come, when, stript of all her charms, 355
The land of scholars, and the nurse of arms,
Where noble stems transmit the patriot flame,
Where kings have toiled, and poets wrote for fame,
One sink of level avarice shall lie,
And scholars, soldiers, kings, unhonored die. 360

Yet think not, thus when freedom's ills I state,
I mean to flatter kings or court the great.
Ye powers of truth, that bid my soul aspire,
Far from my bosom drive the low desire.
And thou, fair Freedom, taught alike to feel 365
The rabble's rage and tyrant's angry steel;
Thou transitory flower, alike undone
By proud contempt, or favor's fostering sun,
Still may thy blooms the changeful clime endure!
I only would repress them to secure: 370
For just experience tells, in every soil,
That those who think must govern those that toil;

And all that freedom's highest aims can reach,
Is but to lay proportioned loads on each.
Hence, should one order disproportioned grow, 375
Its double weight must ruin all below.

O then how blind to all that truth requires,
Who think it freedom when a part aspires !
Calm is my soul, nor apt to rise in arms,
Except when fast-approaching danger warms : 380
But when contending chiefs blockade the throne,
Contracting regal power to stretch their own ;
When I behold a factious band agree
To call it freedom when themselves are free ;
Each wanton judge new penal statutes draw, 385
Laws grind the poor, and rich men rule the law ;
The wealth of climes, where savage nations roam,
Pillaged from slaves to purchase slaves at home ;
Fear, pity, justice, indignation start,
Tear off reserve, and bare my swelling heart ; 390
Till half a patriot, half a coward grown,
I fly from petty tyrants to the throne.

Yes, Brother, curse with me that baleful hour,
When first ambition struck at regal power ;
And thus polluting honor in its source, 395
Gave wealth to sway the mind with double force.
Have we not seen, round Britain's peopled shore,
Her useful sons exchanged for useless ore ?
Seen all her triumphs but destruction haste,
Like flaring tapers brightening as they waste ; 400

Seen opulence, her grandeur to maintain,
Lead stern depopulation in her train,
And over fields where scattered hamlets rose,
In barren solitary pomp repose?
Have we not seen at pleasure's lordly call   405
The smiling long-frequented village fall?
Beheld the duteous son, the sire decayed,
The modest matron and the blushing maid,
Forced from their homes, a melancholy train,
To traverse climes beyond the western main;   410
Where wild Oswego spreads her swamps around,
And Niagara stuns with thundering sound?

Even now, perhaps, as there some pilgrim strays
Through tangled forests, and through dangerous ways,
Where beasts with man divided empire claim,   415
And the brown Indian marks with murderous aim;
There, while above the giddy tempest flies,
And all around distressful yells arise,
The pensive exile, bending with his woe,
To stop too fearful, and too faint to go,   420
Casts a long look where England's glories shine,
And bids his bosom sympathize with mine.

Vain, very vain, my weary search to find
That bliss which only centres in the mind:
Why have I strayed from pleasure and repose,   425
To seek a good each government bestows?

In every government, though terrors reign,
Though tyrant kings, or tyrant laws restrain,
How small, of all that human hearts endure,
That part which laws or kings can cause or cure! 430
Still to ourselves in every place consigned,
Our own felicity we make or find :
With secret course, which no loud storms annoy,
Glides the smooth current of domestic joy.
The lifted axe, the agonizing wheel, 435
Luke's iron crown, and Damiens' bed of steel,
To men remote from power but rarely known,
Leave reason, faith, and conscience, all our own.

PRELIMINARY NOTES.

POETRY.

POETICAL compositions may be variously classified. In respect to form and mode of treatment, they are Epic, Dramatic, or Lyric. With regard to their nature, the principal varieties are, Epic, Dramatic, Lyric, Pastoral, Satirical, Didactic, and Elegiac.

Epic poetry is that variety which treats of some great event, or the exploits of heroes. An heroic poem generally embraces many characters and incidents, but is so constructed as to preserve unity of design.

Dramatic poetry, like Epic, contains the relation of some important events, but differs from it in this, that in Epic poetry the author himself narrates the events forming its subject, but in Dramatic, the action is represented by the different characters from whose dialogues the story is to be gathered.

Lyric poetry is so called because originally written to be sung to the lyre. It now embraces such short, animated poetical compositions as the Ode, Song, Hymn, and Ballad.

Pastoral poetry describes shepherd-life.

Satirical poetry exposes the weaknesses, follies, or crimes of men, and holds them up to ridicule and scorn.

Didactic poetry aims to instruct rather than to please. Being devoted to the exposition or enforcement of some abstract theory, it is dry and uninteresting, unless richly ornamented. Young's *Night Thoughts*, Pope's *Essay on Man*, and Cowper's *Task* are examples of this variety. Goldsmith's *Traveller* may be classed under this head, as it has a proposed theory to enforce.

Elegiac poetry treats of solemn or mournful subjects. Among the few poems of this class in English, are Pope's *Elegy on an Unfortunate Lady*, Tennyson's *In Memoriam*, Wordsworth's *Elegiac Stanzas*, and, best of all, Gray's *Elegy in a Country Church-yard*.

VERSIFICATION.

METRE.—Both the *Traveller* and the *Elegy* are written in Iambic Pentameter measure which is frequently called heroic verse, as it is used in Epic or Heroic poems. Each line consists of five Iambic feet, or ten syllables. An Iambic foot is composed of an unaccented followed by an accented syllable, as *appear*. The *Traveller* is written in rhyming couplets, and the *Elegy* in the quatrain, or stanza of four lines which rhyme alternately. The rhyming couplet in its artificial perfection under Pope became highly epigrammatic, each couplet being, for the most part, complete in itself and often forming a contrast. In the hands of Goldsmith, there are frequent deviations from this strict regularity, which afford the poet greater ease and naturalness in his descriptions.

PAUSES.—There are usually three pauses in each verse ; the *Punctuation* pause which divides the line according to the sense, the *Final* pause which marks the end of each line to the ear, and the *Cæsural* pause which affords a rest for the reader's voice. The cæsural pause is movable, and may occur after the 4th, 5th, 6th, or 7th syllable. Besides the caesural pause there are commonly two other inferior pauses, one before the cæsural, and the other after it. The former invariably comes after the first long syllable ; the other imitates the cæsural pause, coming after the 6th, 7th, or 8th syllable. In the following lines the cæsural pause is marked by double lines, and the secondary pauses each by a single line :

My soul, | turn from them, ‖ turn we | to survey
Where rough|er climes ‖ a nobler race | display,
Where | the bleak Swiss ‖ their storm|y mansion tread,
And force | a churlish soil ‖ for scan|ty bread.

SCANSION.—The *scansion* of verses, or the division into feet, may be indicated in the following manner :

1. Remote', | unfrien'|ded, mel'|anchol'|y, slow':
2. Lakes', for'|ests, cit'|ies, plains' | extend'|ing wide'.
3. Boldly' | proclaims' | that hap'|piest spot' | his own'.
4. And Ni'|aga'|ra stuns' | with thun'|dering sound'.
5. With man'|y a tale' | repays' | his night'|ly bed'.

The first foot of line 2 consists of two syllables naturally long and may therefore be regarded as a spondee. No. 4 is an example of a verse beginning with a trochee instead of an iambus. The extra syllable in line 4 is elided. In line 5 the *y may* either be elided, or the foot regarded as an anapest.

NOTES.

THE TRAVELLER.

EPITOME.

The poet, after expressing the affection which he, while travelling in distant countries, still retains for his brother, invokes a blessing upon that happy home whose comforts he is destined never to share. He fancies himself, in his lonely wanderings, seated on a lofty Alpine peak in the contemplative spirit of a philosopher to moralize on the scene spread out at his feet, not unsympathizingly but philanthropically, rejoicing that the race enjoys so much good though mingled with some remaining ills. From his imaginary seat he looks about him to inquire for the abode of perfect happiness. He finds that every one claims his own land to be that happiest spot; that everywhere man may live and be happy; and that civilization has its drawbacks as well as its advantages. He then proceeds to examine this question as illustrated by the countries which lie around him. In Italy, which possesses the greatest natural advantages, he finds the people vicious, ignorant and degraded; in Switzerland, where the soil is barren and the climate rigorous, the natives are brave and contented, though rude and unrefined; in France the people are idle and easily pleased, seeking praise from one another, but exhibiting little strength of mind or independence of thought; in Holland the very nature of the country has induced habits of industry, industry has led to so sordid a love of gain that the inhabitants are said to exchange anything for money, as the French for praise; in England the climate is mild and moderate, but the people are extreme and independent, independence begets disunion and political strife, and the very liberty which Britons "prize too high" is the cause of much of their unhappiness. The poet here takes occasion, in dilating on the evils of freedom, to introduce reflections of his own on the dangers of England, arising from the undue preponderance of any one class, from the increase of wealth and from the consequent emigration of the "bold peasantry." But the search for perfect happiness has been vain and, indeed, is unimportant, since governments can but little affect the happiness of individuals —that depends on the proper regulation of their own minds.

---

1 Remote, unfriended, melancholy, slow,—attributive adjuncts of *I*, in l. 7. Cf. l. 437.

Melancholy. (Gr. μέλας, black, and χολή, bile) one of a large class of words, used in an old theory of medicine, "according to which there were four principal moistures or humors in the natural body, on the due proportion and combination of which the disposition alike of body and mind depended." See Trench, *Study of Words*, lecture III. Mention other words of the class referred to.

Slow. Boswell, in his *Life of Johnson*, relates the following characteristic incident : "'Chamier,' said Johnson, 'once asked me what he (Goldsmith) meant by *slow*, the last word in the first line of *The Traveller*. Did he mean tardiness of locomotion?' Goldsmith, who would say something without consideration, answered, 'Yes.' I was sitting by, and said, 'No, Sir; you do not mean tardiness of locomotion. You mean that sluggishness of mind which comes upon a man in solitude.' Chamier believed I had written the line as much as if he had seen me write it."

2 Or, by poetic license for *whether*.

Lazy Scheldt. Describe accurately its course; mention, in order, the principal towns and cities upon its banks. Is the epithet *lazy* applicable? Cf. Collins', *Ode to a Lady*.

" By rapid Scheldt's descending wave
 His country's vows shall bless the grave,
 Where'er the youth is laid."

Wandering Po. The Po including its wanderings is upwards of 450 miles long. From its rise to its mouth is only 270 miles, in a straight line.

3 Where the rude, etc. An adverbial clause, qualifying the adverb *onward*.

Rude. What does *rude* mean here?

Carinthia. A province of Austria, between Illyria and Styria, probably visited by G. during his tour on the continent.

THE TRAVELLER.   47

2-3 These lines form what is called an *assonance*, i.e. 'a correspondence of sound in the termination of verses less complete than that of rhyme.' It is frequently, as here, a rhyming to the eye, but not to the ear.

Boor. A. S. *gebure*, a farmer, from *buan*, to till. Dutch *boer*, a husbandman. Many words, of which this is a good example, have become degraded in meaning.

"No word would illustrate this process better than that old example familiar probably to us all, of 'villain.' The 'villain' is, first, the serf or peasant, 'villanus,' because attached to the 'villa' or farm. He is, secondly, the peasant who, it is further taken for granted, will be churlish, selfish, dishonest, and generally of evil moral conditions, these having come to be assumed as always belonging to him, and to be permanently associated with his name, by those higher classes of society, the καλοί κα'γαθοί, who in the main commanded the springs of language. At the third step, nothing of the meaning which the etymology suggests, nothing of 'villa,' survives any longer; peasant is wholly dismissed, and the evil moral conditions of him who is called by this name alone remain; so that the name would now in this its final stage be applied as freely to peer, if he deserved it, as to peasant. 'Boor' has had exactly the same history; being first the cultivator of the soil; then secondly, the cultivator of the soil, who, it is assumed, will be coarse, rude, and unmannerly; and then thirdly, any one who is coarse, rude, and unmannerly."—Trench's *English Past and Present*, lect. VII.

5 Campania. "Campagna di Roma, an undulating, uncultivated, and unhealthy plain of Italy surrounding Rome, including the greatest part of ancient Latium. The ground, which never rises more than 200 feet above the sea, is almost entirely volcanic and the lakes are formed by craters of extinct volcanoes. The number of inhabitants is very small, and in summer they are driven from the sea by its pestilent air, and seek shelter in Rome and other neighboring places. This district was not always uncultivated and depopulated as we now find it, for Domitian and Hadrian built here their splendid villas.—Chambers's *Encyclopædia*.

Forsaken. Complement of the predicate *lies*.

6 Waste. A secondary complement of *lies*,—in the predicate nominative.

7 After *realms* supply *I roam*. The clause is concessive adverbial, qualifying *turns*.

9 My brother. The Rev. Henry Goldsmith to whom this poem is dedicated. He was the eldest of the family, and his father's favorite. In his collegiate career, he greatly distinguished himself, winning a scholarship in the year 1743. But, with the improvidence of his race, he, during the succeeding vacation, married for love, gave up his collegiate course, and began to teach a school. This, he continued for a short time, but soon received the curacy of Lissoy, at forty pounds a year. Here he spent the remainder of his life, in great domestic comfort and in the enjoyment of the love and affection of all his parishioners.

Explain *pain* here, and compare it with pain in l. 15.

10 Cf. Citizen of the World, letter III., where he had previously used this beautiful and affecting image. "The farther I travel I feel the pain of separation with stronger force. Those ties that bind me to my native country and you, are still unbroken; by every remove I only drag a greater length of chain."

11 Crown. This may be regarded as the third person of the imperative, or as the subjunctive used optatively. See Abbott's *How to Parse*, par. 504.

15 Want and pain, by metonymy for persons suffering from 'want and pain.'

16 And every stranger, etc. Supply *where*. The clause is adjectival to *abode*.

18 Around=who gather around the board. It is to be taken as an adjective qualifying *family*.

19 That never fail. That are never wanting among children, or, possibly, it may mean, that never fail to provoke merriment.

Several poets have given us descriptions of the ideal clergyman. See Wordsworth's *Excursion*, Bk. V.; Dryden's *Character of a Parson*, imitated from the *Prologue* to Chaucer's *Canterbury Tales;* Cowper's *Task*, Bk. II.; and particularly the *Deserted Village*, ll. 137-192.

21 What is the subject of *press?* Cf. *D. V.*, l. 149.

" His house was known to all the vagrant train,
He chid their wanderings, but relieved their pain."

22 And learn, etc. This clause, like each of the three preceding, is adjectival to *feasts*.

Doing is a participial noun in the objective case after *of*. *Good* is a noun, objective case after *doing*.

THE TRAVELLER. 49

23 Me. The object of *leads* in l. 29.

24 Prime is in the nominative absolute.

25 Impelled, etc., like *destined*, etc., forms an attributive adjunct of *me*.

27 Like. According to the common parsing, *like* is here an adverb qualifying *allures*, and *circle* is in the objective after *to* understood. But this is clearly wrong. The poet does not mean that the manner of alluring resembles a circle, i.e., that an action resembles a line; but he intends to say, that this *fleeting good* allures him on, in a manner similar to that in which the horizon *(the circle bounding earth and skies)* allures the traveller on. Hence the correct parsing is, *like* is a conjunctive adverb, and *circle* is the subject of *allures* understood.

See Earle's *Philology*, par. 220, and Angus's *Handbook*, par. 322.

28 Far is to be taken as a noun, in the objective after *from*.

(That) *yet flies* is an adjectival clause qualifying *good*. *Yet* is an adverb qualifying *flies*.

As I follow is adverbial to *flies*.

29 Alone is the complement of the verb of incomplete predication, *traverse*, and is to be parsed as an adjective qualifying *me*.

30 My own is the objective complement of *find*, and as an adjective qualifies *spot*.

32 I sit me. *Sit* is now intransitive. The use of archaic forms adds dignity to poetry.

34 An hundred. Cf. *D. V.*, 93, "an hare," *an* is another form of *one*. Cf. Scotch, *ane*.

The distinction we make with regard to the use of *an* and *a* is only a modern innovation. In old and middle English *an* was almost invariably used.

35 Lakes, etc., are in apposition to *an hundred realms*.

36 The pomp of kings seems intended as the appositive to *lakes, forests, cities;* and *shepherd's humbler pride*, to *plains*.

Wide is an adjective qualifying *plains*.

37 What part of speech is *around?* See note on l. 18.

40 Vain is the objective complement of *makes*.

See Rushton, sec. 16. By Abbott, this is called the *objective supplement*. See *How to Parse*, par. 149. Explain *vain* here.

41 School-taught. This epithet should not, as some

have supposed, be confined either to the Stoic or Mediæval Philosophy; but is to be understood to mean scholastic doctrine generally.

Dissemble is the complement of the verb of incomplete predication *let*. By some this is called the *complementary infinitive*, completing the object *world*. See *How to Parse*, par. 97.

All—as much as.

42 Man. Account for the poet's having written *man* here.

43 Sympathetic. Gr. σύν, together, πάθος, feeling. Possessing fellow-feeling.

44 Exult. Lat. *ex*, and *saltare*, to leap.

45, 48 Point out the figures in these lines.

47 Busy, as employed to propel so many vessels. What figure in *busy?*

48 Bending=stooping to their work.

Dress. Lat. *dirigere*, to put straight; It. *drizzare*, to raise; Fr. *dresser*, to make straight.

50 Heir. Before *creation's* supply *I being*. Absolute case, forming extension of the succeeding proposition.

Mine, a pronoun in the possessive case, the complement of *is*; or simply an adjective, (Lat. *meus*), the complement of *is*. Latham, chap. 37, strongly maintains the latter view.

51-52 "Rhyme speaks to the ear, and not to the eye. If, therefore, the concluding sound is the same, no matter what the spelling, the rhyme is perfect." This is the case with this couplet.

51-56 Arrange these lines thus :—*As hoards after hoards fill his (some lone miser's) rising raptures (while) some lone miser (he) visiting his store, bends at his treasure, counts, recounts it o'er; (and as) yet he still sighs, for hoards are wanting still: thus to my breast alternate passions rise, (I being) pleased with each good that Heaven to man supplies.*

55 Passions. What does *passions* mean here? Compare its meaning in this line with its etymological, and with its usual sense.

56 Each, here, as in various other lines, is used for every. Cf. 1. 61.

57 Sorrows. What figure?

58 To see, etc. An adverbial adjunct of *fall*.

61 Hope. Nominative absolute.

62 To see=on seeing, and is an adverbial adjunct of *may gather*.

THE TRAVELLER.

63 Where *(we are) to find, etc.*, is a noun clause object of *can direct* (=can tell).
Below—*on the earth*, and is an adverb qualifying *to find*.
64 How does the meaning of *tenant* here differ from its usual signification?
67 Enumerate the principal *treasures of his stormy seas*.
68 Long nights. Give their length at the Arctic circle, and also at a point midway between it and the pole.
Revelry. What is the meaning of this word here? Shew how far, in its ordinary sense, it is applicable to the habits of polar races.
69 Line. What is meant?
70 Golden sands. Is there any good reason for supposing that the Gold Coast is particularly referred to?
Palmy wine. Wine made from the sap of the palm tree.
72 Gods. What gods are meant?
Point out the grammatical error in this line, and account for it. Cf. l. 113, and *D. V.*, l. 92.
"Where Mahommedanism has not been introduced, the religion of the negroes is nothing but a debased *fetish* worship. They make fetishes of serpents, elephants' teeth, tigers' claws, and other parts of animals, at the dictation of their *fetish man*, or priest. They also manufacture idols of wood and stone, which they worship; and yet, under all this, they have some idea of a Supreme Being."—Chambers's *Encyclopædia*.
74 His first .. home. This is a noun clause in apposition to *boast*.
80 Even is the objective complement of *makes*, and as an adjective qualifies *blessings*.
82 Bliss=favors.
83 Peasant. Fr. *paysan*, one living in the country, from *pays*, country; Lat. *pagus*, a district. What other word does G. use as a synonym of *peasant*?
84 Idra or rather Idria, a small but important town of Austria in the crownland of Carniola, celebrated for its quicksilver mines, is situated in a deep caldron-shaped valley on a river of the same name, 22 miles south-west of Laibach.
Arno. Trace its course. What towns on its banks?
After *as*, supply *he is supplied on (Arno's shelvy side).*
Shelvy=rising with gentle shelf-like ridges.

86 Custom. Lat. *consuesco*, to be accustomed. Old Fr *coustume.* Fr. *coutume.*

88 Content. Cf. *Macbeth*, III. 2 :
"Nought's had, all's spent,
Where our desire is got without content."

89 Each other's. *Each*, a distributive pronoun in apposition to subject *these*. Some writers seem to regard 'each other' as a compound pronoun.

See *How to Parse*, pars. 223, 385, 531; Dr. Adams, par. 258; Cf. Pope :

"O'er the pale marble shall they join their heads
And drink the falling tears each other sheds."

Strong=strongly.

90 Either. *Each* would be the proper word here, as *either* refers to one of two objects, not to one of five.

Destructive is the complement of *seems*.

91-92 Inquire into the truth of these assertions.

97 Carried .. domain. This clause forms an attributive adjunct of the subject *good*.

Domain. What is meant by *domain* here?

98 Peculiar pain. Means the pain which arises from pursuing *this favorite good*. Distinguish peculiar and particular. Cf. Gray's *Ode on the Pleasure of Vicissitude:*
"Still where rosy pleasure leads
See a kindred grief pursue."

99 Try may be regarded as the complement of *let*.

These truths. What *truths?*

100 Through the prospect as it lies. Through the different countries which lie before the poet.

101 My proper cares=my own cares. *Cares* is nominative absolute.

103 Like yon .. cast. *Like* is here an adjective qualifying *me*. *Yon* is a demonstrative adjective. There is in this expression a melancholy reference to his own friendless condition.

105 Far qualifies the phrase *to the right*.

Apennine. Why not Apennines? Trace this mountain chain on the map. Cf. Byron's *Childe Harold*, canto IV :

"Once more upon the woody Apennine,
The infant Alps."

THE TRAVELLER. 53

106 Bright is an adjective qualifying *Italy* and forms the complement of *extends*.

107 By uplands are to be understood successive terraces on the mountain side which are covered by "woods over woods."

108 Woods over woods. The first *woods* is in the nominative absolute.

The wooded uplands rise one above another like the rows of boxes at a theatre.

109 After *tops* supply *which stand out between these woods*. Without supplying, *between* may be parsed as an adjective, since it takes the place of an adjectival clause.

While .. scene. This proposition is co-ordinate with the preceding, since *while* merely continues the description.

110 Mark. Give the exact meaning of this word here.

111 Cf. Virgil's *Georgics*, II. 136–176; Roger's *Italy*; Byron's *Childe Harold*, canto IV.; also, Addison's *Letter from Italy*, where he says:

" How has kind heaven adorned the land,
And scattered blessings with a wasteful hand !
But what avail her unexhausted stores,
Her blooming mountains and her sunny shores,
With all the gifts that heaven and earth impart,
The smiles of nature, and the charms of art,
While proud oppression in the valleys reigns,
And tyranny usurps her happy plains ?"

112 Were=would be. Subjunctive used for potential by enallage.

113 Whatever .. found. This clause and the clauses forming ll. 115 to 117, are each noun propositions forming the subject of *own* in l. 119. The form is similar to: "whatever is, is best."

Correct the grammatical error in this line.

114 Mention some of the 'fruits' that 'proudly rise' or 'humbly court the ground.'

118 What is meant by *vernal lives ?*

But, an adverb qualifying *to die*.

119 These is in apposition to the noun clauses of ll. 113, 115 and 117.

Explain *kindred soil*. Is *the* correct here ?

121 Parse *while*. See note on l. 109.

Gelid wings. Why *gelid* ?

THE TRAVELLER.

Point out all the figures of speech in ll. 111-122.

123 Sense=senses. So *sensual*, as opposed to intellectual.

125 Florid beauty, i.e., beauty produced by profusion of flowers.

126 His manners, not only his outward actions, but his character. Cf. Lat. *mores*.

128 Though poor, luxurious. Supply *he is*, and read: *He is luxurious, though he is poor*.

129 Zealous, yet untrue. In order to make this contrast clear, *zealous* must be taken to mean, professedly ardent, and *untrue*, to signify practically unfaithful.

130 Even, an adverb, qualifying the phrase *in penance*. For analysis, supply *he is* with *planning*.

131 Contaminate. Lat. *contamen*, for *contagimen*, contact; *con*, with, and *tango*, to touch. Give synonyms, and compare them.

133 Date is nominative absolute; and the clause *not far . . date* forms an adverbial extension of *was*. *Date* is the time when any document is *given* or issued. Cf. the expression: '*Given* under our hand, etc.'

134 Florence, Pisa, Genoa, Venice, and some other Italian towns, acquired great wealth by their extensive commerce in the middle ages, and the people became intelligent and refined: but jealousies arising between these independent republics led to disastrous wars which, aided by civil dissensions, ended in the ruin of their power and the destruction of their commerce.

135 The palace, etc. The splendid mansions of the merchant princes of the commercial towns.

These imposing structures are now mostly uninhabited; those that are occupied, being chiefly used as hotels.

136 The long-fallen column, etc. 'That is, since the old Roman days.' "The first modern sculptor of any note, and the true father of modern sculpture, was Nicolo Pisano, an artist of the thirteenth century. Among his successors, the most eminent were Andrea Pisano and Andrea Orcagna of the fourteenth; and Lucca della Robbia, Lorenzo Ghiberti, Donatello, and Brunelleschi, of the fifteenth century. In the fifteenth and sixteenth centuries, Italy was full of artists, many of whom were at once architects, painters, and sculptors, as Michael Angelo and Cellini."—Chambers's *Mediæval Hist.*

137 Canvas. Painting began to revive in Italy under Guido of Tuscany, 1221. Among his successors were Giotto of Florence, Fra Angelico (1389), Masaccio (1401), Lippi (1416), Gozzoli, Perugino (1446), Bellini of Venice (1426). The climax of Italian art was attained in the generation immediately succeeding that of these painters, when Leonardi da Vinci, Michael Angelo, Raphael, Titian, and Sanzio D'Urbino lived.

Warm is an attributive adjunct of *canvas*.

E'en. Parse *e'en*. See note on l. 130.

138 Explain this line.

139 Southern gale. Why does the poet say *southern gale* rather than any other?

The causes of the decay of Italian commerce are to be sought; in the exhausting warfare which destroyed the shipping and crippled the resources, now of one city, now of another; in the discovery of America; and in that of the sea-route to India.

141 For the parsing of *while*, see note on l. 109.

Gave. The sequence of tenses requires *had given*.

Riches is etymologically of the singular number, but is plural in form, and the form appears to account for its being used with a plural verb.

142 But towns unmanned and (but) lords without a slave, are adverbial extensions of the verb *remained*, as they=if we except towns, etc. *But* is here a preposition.

Unmanned=uninhabited.

143 Skill=knowledge. From A. S. *scylan*, to distinguish.

144 Former. The old English *for-m-a* signifies *first*, the superlative of a root *fore*. *Fyrmest*=*for-m-ost* also had the same meaning, but is a double superlative. Former is a comparative formed from the old superlative.

But=only.

Plethoric. Plethora, from Gr. $\pi\lambda\eta\theta\acute{u}\omega$, to be full, signifies in medicine an overfulness of blood. Hence by 'plethoric ill' the poet means that the unwonted activity which the increase of commerce, and consequently of wealth, had produced, was not a natural outcome of genuine national health; but that its 'former strength' was not, as had been supposed, real strength at all, but merely an outward appearance of it, brought on by a superfluity of wealth, as an overfulness of blood in the body induces over-exertion.

146 Wrecks. The arts as now cultivated in Italy are as wrecks compared with the productions of the great masters of former ages.

THE TRAVELLER.

150 Pasteboard triumph.
This seems to refer to some of the out-door amusements practised during the Carnival, particularly at Venice and Rome. "The carriage and horses are decked out in a very fine or a very capricious manner. A coachman, dressed as a Spanish cavalier of the olden times, is driving an old Tabellone, or notary, with a huge wine-flask (extended towards a Punch on stilts), and a Roman doctor, with 'spectacles on nose,' while a small-grown Punch climbs up the side steps, and Punchinello, with a squeaking trumpet to his lips, and a sturdy turbaned Moor act as footmen."—See McFarlane's *Popular Customs of the South of Italy*.

Cavalcade. Gr. καβάλλης, a pack-horse; Lat. *caballus*, a horse; It. *cavalcata*, a cavalcade.

"This probably refers to the Races at Rome during the Carnival. The horses are without riders, but have spurs, sheets of tin, and all sorts of things hung about them to urge them onward; across the end of the Piazzo de Popolo is stretched a rope, in a line with which the horses are brought up; in a second or two, the rope is let go, and away the horses fly at a fearful rate down the Corso, which is crowded with people, among whom the plunging and kicking of the steeds often produce serious damage."—Chambers's *Encyclopædia*.

151 Processions is the subject of *may be seen* understood, as are also *mistress* and *saint*.

153-154 "Sir Joshua Reynolds calling upon the poet one day, opened the door without ceremony, and found him in the double occupation of turning a couplet, and teaching a pet dog to sit upon his haunches. At one time he would glance his eye at his desk, and at another, shake his finger at the dog to make him retain his position. These lines form the couplet and were still wet. Goldsmith, with his usual good humor, joined in the laugh caused by his whimsical employment, and acknowledged that his boyish sport with the dog suggested the thought."—Irving's *Life of Goldsmith*.

154 What figure in this line?

155 Represt. The *e* of the weak, unaccented syllable *ed* is often dropped in conversation, so that the word loses its additional syllable, and we are forced to pronounce a *t* instead of a *d*. In attempting to pronounce, in one syllable, a *surd* and a *sonant*, either the surd will become a sonant, or the sonant will become a surd. Thus *sofd* will become either *sovd* or *soft*. So *d* will pass into *t* after *p*, *sh*, *s* sharp, *x*, *ch* and *ck*.

157 Fast behind=closely behind.

159 *While low delights* (so) *occupy the mind in happier meanness; as the shelter-seeking peasant heedless of the dead builds his shed there in the ruin, in those domes defaced by time and tottering in decay, where Cæsars once bore sway; and,* (as he) *wondering man could want the larger pile, exults, and* (as he) *owns his cottage with a smile.* This arrangement makes the analysis clear, although the construction is somewhat loose, and the simile not carefully carried out.

Domes from Lat. *domus*, a house, has here its familiar poetic meaning of a high and spacious hall. Cf. *D. V.*, 319.

"The dome where pleasure holds her midnight reign."

Cæsars, here, probably, means noble and wealthy Romans generally. What figure? Who were the Cæsars, in the sense of Emperors?

164 Cottage. Called *shed* in l. 162.

165 Turn we. *Turn* is 1st person, plural, imperative.

Survey. From Latin, *super*, over, and *video*, to see; O. Fr. *surveoir*; Fr. *sur*, over, above, and *voir*, to see.

166 Where . . display. This is a substantive clause, the object of *survey*.

167 Bleak, akin to *bleach* is here applied, as it originally was, to persons. It is now usually applied to places.

Mansion. From Lat. *manere*, to remain, to abide. Compare the meaning of *mansion* here with the sense in which it is used in l. 201, and in ll. 140, 195, 238 of the *D. V.*

168 And force, etc. A most happy line, expressive of the difficulty of wringing from the barren soil its scanty produce.

Churlish. A. S. *ceorl*, a country-man. The word is generally applied to persons, but sometimes to things. See note on l. 3.

170 But man . . sword. This clause is adverbial to *afford*. See note on l. 142.

Soldier is in apposition to *man;* and *sword*, to *steel*.

One might be led to suppose from the reading of this line that there are iron mines in Switzerland; this, however, is not the case.

What ground is there for inferring, as some have done, that G. here alludes to the fact, that 'from the 15th century, the Swiss were the chief mercenary soldiers of Europe'?

Cf. *Hamlet*, IV. 5: "Where are my Switzers"? and Scott, *Lady of the Lake*, VI. 3:

"The mountain-loving Switzer there
More freely breathed in mountain-air."

171. Torpid. Lat. *torpeo*, I am benumbed.

Array. It. *arredo*, furniture or implements; Sp. *arreo*, dress; Fr. *arroi*, equipage.

173 Sues. Lat. *sequor*, Fr. *suis*, I follow.

Cf. Scott, *Lady of the Lake*:

"Just kissed the lake, just stirred the trees."

174 Meteors. Gr. μετέωρα, things in the air; μετά, noting direction, and αἰώρα, a hovering in the air. This word has particular reference in this case to the lightning so frequent and vivid in mountainous countries.

176 Redress. What was the original meaning of this word? What sense does it bear in l. 214?

178 The lot of all. *Lot* in this phrase is in apposition to the preceding *lot*.

179 Rear is the complement of *sees*. See note on l. 292.

Contiguous palace. Cf. *D. V.*, l. 304:

"Where then, ah! where shall poverty reside,
To 'scape the pressure of contiguous pride!"

181 Supply *He sees* before *no costly*, etc.

Costly. Explain this word. What figure?

Banquet. Fr. *banquet*; It. *benchetto*; Ger. *bankett*, from *bank*, a bench or table at which messmates sit and feast together.

183 Calm, bred . . toil and each . . contracting, are attributive adjuncts of *he*, understood, the subject of *fits*.

184 Him is a personal pronoun used reflexively, for himself. Cf. ll. 32 and 192. Paraphrase *fits him to the soil*.

185 Cheerful is the complement of *wakes*.

186 Breasts. "This is the reading of all the early editions, and Johnson quotes it in his *Dict.* as an illustration of the verb. The reading 'Breathes,' found in the *Globe* ed., doubtless had its origin in a misprint."

Carols. It. *carolare*, to sing; *carola*, a kind of dance; O. Fr. *carolle*; W. *carol*, a love-song.

187 Patient angle. It is not the *angle*, but the angler that is patient. "This figure is not dignified with a proper name, because it has been overlooked by writers."—Lord Kames' *Elements of Criticism.*

Angle is now seldom used as a noun. See Shak., *A. and C.*, II. 5: "Give me mine angle; we'll to the river."

Trolls. Ger. *trollen*, to roll. "To fish, as for pikes, with a rod, the line of which runs on a reel, or to fish by letting the line drag through the water."

Finny deep. Same figure as in *patient angle*, and in *venturous ploughshare* in the next line.

Cf. *D. V.*, l. 361, and Gray's *Elegy*, sta. 6, "blazing hearth."

188 Savage. Lat. *silva*, a wood; *silvaticus*, an inhabitant of the woods; It. *selvaggio;* Fr. *sauvage*. Here probably means the bear. Cf. *Cit. of World*, I.: "Drive the reluctant savage into the toils." As a substantive, we now apply *savage* only to human beings.

191 Every labor sped. Labor is nominative absolute. *Sped*=accomplished.

192 Monarch is in the predicate nominative, and may be taken as the complement of the verb of incomplete predication *sits*. See note on l. 32.

193 Smiles, etc. Cf. Gray's *Elegy*, sta. 6.

197 And haply too, etc. This is a principal proposition. **Haply**=perchance.

198 Scan this line.

Many a tale. This is a more than ordinarily difficult construction. Archbishop Trench in the first editions of his *English Past and Present*, explained "many a man" as a corruption of "many of men." In the later editions he has quietly withdrawn this statement. Many very excellent grammarians, such as Fleming, Dr. Adams, Rushton, have adopted his solution without due examination. In early English it was a frequent practice to emphasize the adjective by a change of position, as *long a time*, for *a long time*. This is shown by our retention of such expressions as *such a woman, what a day.* In Layamon, I. 24: "*On moni* are wisen" *(later text* mani ane); "*monianes* cunnes" *ib.* 39; of *many a kind.* Abbott's *Shakespearian Gram.* par. 85. Abbott in his *How to Parse*, par. 218, says the regular construction for *many a man has tried* would be *many men have tried;* but this appears to have been confused with "many times a man has tried." Hence Abbott parses *many* as an adverb modifying *a* or as part of the compound adjective *many-a*= *many-one*=A. S. *mani-an*.

Other authorities regard *many* as an adjective, and the construction as inverted. See Mason, par. 93; Dr. Adams, par. 571; Angus, sec. 480; Rushton, pars. 281, 299-302.

Nightly=for the night. Cf. Milton, *Il Pens*, 84:

"To bless the doors from nightly harm."

200 Patriot passion, love for his native country.

201 Even is joined to *those ills* for the purpose of emphasis.

202 Enhance. Lat. *ante*, before; Fr. *en avant;* Provençal, *enansar*, to forward.

203 Conforms=accommodates itself.

205 As a child clings close and closer to the mother's breast is adverbial to *bind*. The construction is clear if *binds itself* is substituted for *clings*; thus, *The loud torrent . . but bind him . . shore, as the child binds itself (clings) to the mother's breast.*

206 Close and closer=closer and closer. Cf. *M. for M.* IV. 6: "The soft and sweetest music."

208 But=only, an adverb, qualifying *bind*.

What part of speech is *more*?

211 Let is a verb of incomplete predication, *them* is the object, and *share*, the complement. See note on l. 41.

What does *share* mean here?

213 Explain stimulates. Does the poet mean that every want that is felt in a barren country is supplied?

215 Whence=for these reasons, or in consequence of these facts.

216 And then supplies=and then gratifies the desires which it has excited.

217 Sensual pleasures, the pleasures arising from the senses, as opposed to intellectual. Cf. *sensual bliss* in l. 124.

When . . cloy. A noun clause in apposition to *it*.

218 What is meant by *languid pause?* By *finer joy?*

221 Level=monotonous, as consisting in little more than "forcing a churlish soil for scanty bread." Cf. Mrs. Browning:

"We miss far prospects by a level bliss."

222 Unquenched by want and unfanned by strong desire are adjuncts of *fire*.

Unquenched. A. S. *un*, not, and *cwencan*, to quench.

223 (The vulgar breast is) *unfit for raptures, or, if rap-*

tures cheer on some high festival of once a year, (it) *(the vulgar breast) takes fire in wild excess, till,* (it) *buried in debauch, the bliss expire.*

224 Of once a year. This whole phrase is adjectival to *festival.* *Once* is a substantive, and is qualified by the phrase, *(in) a year.*

226 Debauch. Old Fr. *bauche,* a row of bricks.

Buried in debauch. This is an absolute phrase forming an adverbial extension of *expire.*

Expire. Account for this subjunctive form. Would it be correct in prose?

227 Not their joys alone thus coarsely flow. = *It is not their joys alone that thus coarsely flow.* *Not* does not qualify flow.

228 Like their pleasures forms an adverbial clause, qualifying *low.* It is not asserted that *their morals* are *like their pleasures,* but that *their morals are low* in the same manner as *their pleasures* are. For *like* see note on l. 27.

230 Unaltered and **unimproved** are complements of *run.* See *How to Parse,* par. 148-150.

232 Fall is not grammatically correct, but may be explained as an instance of "construction according to sense."

Blunted is the complement of *fall.*

Indurated. Lat. *durare,* to harden; and *in,* used intensively.

234 Like=as, is here a conjunctive adverb. See note on l. 27.

Falcons is the subject of *may sit* understood, and *cowering* is the complement.

Cowering, here means simply, brooding, with no notion of fear. Cf. Dryden:

"Our dame sits cowering o'er a kitchen fire."

235 As play . . walks, and (as) **charm the way.** These clauses are each adjectival; *as* performing the office of a relative pronoun. See *How to Parse,* par. 205.

237 These, i.e., the gentler morals. *These* is in apposition to *morals.*

241 Sprightly. Spright, or sprite is a contraction for spirit. *Esprit* is from the same root, Lat. *spirare,* to breathe.

243 Choir. Gr. $\chi o \rho c's$, a dance; Lat. *chorus;* Fr. *chœur;* A. S. *chor.* It here has its original meaning. Cf. *V. of W.*

"I had some knowledge of music, with a tolerable voice; I now turned what was once my amusement into a present means of subsistence. I passed among the harmless peasants of Flanders, and among such of the French as were poor enough to be merry; for I ever found them sprightly in proportion to their wants. Whenever I approached a peasant's house, towards nightfall, I played one of my merriest tunes, and that procured me not only a lodging, but subsistence for the next day; but in truth I must own, whenever I attempted to entertain persons of a higher rank, they always thought my performance odious, and never made me any return for my endeavors to please them."

244 Tuneless, because it *but mocked all tune, and marred the dancer's skill.*

Loire. Trace minutely the course of this river, noting the Departments through which it flows, and the chief towns and cities on its banks.

245 Where . . grew is an adverbial clause to *led*.

246 Supply *where* before *freshened*. *Freshened* is the complement of *flew*.

247 Haply qualifies *would praise* and *would dance*.

Faltering. Gr. σφάλλω, to make fall; Lat. *fallo*, to deceive; It. *faltare*, to be wanting. Compare its meaning here with its ordinary signification.

248 But=only.

Skill. Distinguish the meaning of *skill* in this line from that which it bears in l. 143. Compare also *skill* in l. 90, *D. V.*

249 Village=villagers by metonymy.

250 Forgetful, etc., is an adjunct of the subject of *dance*.

251 Alike all ages. Persons of all ages are alike, *i.e.*, old and young.

Dames of ancient days=elderly women.

252 Have led. Is this tense grammatically correct? Compare l. 254. When should the present perfect be used?

253 Gestic lore. Gestic from the Latin *gero*, *gestus*, is here closely connected in meaning with gesture and gesticulation. His *gestic lore* means his skill in dancing. Cf. Scott, *Peveril of the Peak*: "He seemed, like herself, carried away by the enthusiasm of the gestic art."

256 Idly busy, an example of oxymoron. Cf. Horace's "Strenua nos exercet inertia," and Pope's

"Life's idle business at one gasp be o'er."

THE TRAVELLER.

World=their life in this world.

257 Theirs. See note on l. 50.

258 Honor. See ll. 259 and 260 for the definition of this so-called *honor*.

20 Even is joined to *imaginary worth* in order to emphasize it.

261 Current is the complement of *passes*.

Paid from hand to hand. What part of the sentence is this?

262 Traffic. It. *traffic*; Fr. *trafic*; from Lat. *trans*, beyond, and *facere*, to do.

Explain *splendid traffic*.

264 Avarice is the direct *retained object* after the verb in the passive voice. See *How to Parse*, pars. 117, 122 and 123. Cf. Horace, *Ars Poetica*, 324: "Praeter laudem nullus avarus."

266 What they seem is a noun clause after *to*. Parse *what*.

268 To rise is used adjectively. See *How to Parse*, par. 109.

270 Internal strength of thought. Goldsmith seems to have been ignorant of the works of leading French authors of his time, as Diderot, Voltaire, d' Alembert, Beaumarchais, and Rousseau.

273 Tawdry. "This word is said to be formed by contraction from Ethelred, and applied originally to laces and similar articles sold at the fairs of St. Ethel..l."—*Richardson*. "A vulgar corruption of St. Audrey, or Auldrey, meaning St. Ethelred."—*Nares*. See note on l. 3. Cf. Prior:

"And laying by her tawdry vest."

276 Frieze. Sp. *frisa*; Fr. *frise*; W. *ffris*;—perhaps so called from the Frisians.

277 Cheer. Give meaning.

278 To boast=to boast of.

Once qualifies the phrase *a year*. *Year* is the objective case.

After **banquet** some such word as *given* may be supplied. The whole clause *once a year* forms an adjunct of *banquet*.

280 What is the meaning of *self-applause* here?

281 Other, an adjective=different.

282 Embosomed is the complement of *lies*, and is parsed a past participle referring to *Holland*.

283 Her patient . . stand is a noun clause, the subject of *thinks* in *methinks*, and *me* is the dative case=*to me*. Thinks is from A. S. *thincan*, to seem, not from *thencan*, to think. See *How to Parse*, par. 328, and Rushton, sec. 166.

284 Leans against, etc. Cf. Dryden—

"And view the ocean leaning on the sky."

285 Sedulous, from Lat. *sedeo*, I sit,=sitting close to work, diligent. The phrase *sedulous* . . *tide* is an adjunct of *they*, understood, the subject of *lift*.

Artificial pride. Explain this.

286 Lift . . pride, the construction is the same as in l. 283.

Rampire. This is another form of rampart which is from Lat. *re*, again, *im*, in, and *parare*, to prepare. Cf. Dryden's *Æneid*, VII. 213:

"The Trojans round the place a rampire cast."

287 Diligently slow. This phrase is beautifully expressive of the vast amount of persevering toil necessary to build these immense dykes.

288 The firm . . grow. For the construction of this clause, and the three succeeding, see note on l. 283.

Firm, an adverb=firmly, qualifying *connected*.

Bulwark. Dutch, *bolwork;* Ger. *bollwerk:* Fr. *boulevard*.

"These ramparts are in appearance long green mounds, broad at the base, graduated in their slope, and often of sufficient width to admit of a canal or road, or both, being formed along the top. To give strength to the fabric, willows are planted and also interwoven like wicker-work on the sides. Carried along the banks of rivers, and in some places along the margin of the sea, as well as crosswise in different parts of Holland, a singular net-work of embanking is presented, which answers the double purpose of a protection from inundation and a means of having canals, by which superfluous water pumped from the meadows, or *polders*, may be run off into the sea. The whole system of dyking is placed under local and general superintendence, at a considerable cost to the public. One of the most gigantic of these dykes is that along the Helder; it measures about six miles in length, 40 feet broad at the summit, along which there is a good road, and descends into the sea by a slope of 200 feet, inclined about 40 degrees."—Chambers's *Encyclopædia*.

THE TRAVELLER. 65

To grow is the complement of *seem*. See note on l. 41.

291 While the pent, etc. Cf. the *Animated Nature*, where G. says : " The whole kingdom of Holland seems to be a conquest on the sea, and in a manner rescued from its bosom. The surface of the earth in this country is below the level of the bed of the sea ; and I remember upon approaching the coast to have looked down upon it from the sea as into a valley."

292 Smile is the complement of *sees*. See note on l. 41.

293 Canals. "Canals are more numerous in Holland than in any other country. They there form the chief means of transport. Those of most importance to the national trade are, the North Holland Canal, connecting Amsterdam with the North Sea ; the Voorne Canal, from the north side of Voorne to Hellevoetslins ; the South Villemsvaart, through North Brabant, Dutch and Belgian Limburg, from Hertogenbosch to Maastricht, being 71½ English miles in length, and having 24 locks."—Chambers's *Encyclopædia*.

Yellow-blossomed vale. How is *vale* applied here? Explain *yellow-blossomed*. Give rules for the proper use of hyphens.

294 Willow-tufted. See note on l. 288.

Sail=ship by synecdoche.

295 Mart, a contraction of *market*. A. S. *market*. Cf. Dutch and Ger. *markt;* Mod. Lat. *mercheta;* Lat. *mercatus* from *merces*, goods ; Fr. *marché*.

296 Creation is a summing up of *canal, vale, bank, sail, mart,* and *plain*, and is in the objective case in apposition to these words, as they are to *world*.

297 Around=hereabouts, in this country.

Wave-subjected probably refers to the land having been so long under the sea, that it has become covered with sand, and consequently unproductive.

300 Begets. Give the various uses of *be* in composition.

301 With all those ills, etc. *Those ills* are largely dwelt on in the *D. V.*, which see from l. 265 to the end.

302 Are. Grammatically, the plural cannot be justified here.—See Adams, par. 596. Some consider that it may be allowed as an example of 'construction according to sense'. Others contend that *with* is equal to *and*.

305 After *but* supply *if*, or *view* may be considered the imperative.

A 5

Craft. A. S. *cræft*, art, or trade. For degradation of meaning see note on l. 3.

306 Even. See note on l. 260.

Cf. *V. of W.*, ch. XIX.: "Now the possessor of accumulated wealth, when furnished with the necessaries and pleasures of life, has no other method to employ the superfluity of his fortune but in purchasing power, by purchasing the liberty of the needy or the venal, of men who are willing to bear the mortification of contiguous tyranny for bread."

309 Land and den are in the nominative absolute. Cf. *Citizen of the World:* "A nation once famous for setting the world an example of freedom is now become a land of tyrants and a den of slaves."

Cf. Scott:

"And doubly dying shall go down
To the vile dust from whence they sprung."

312 Dull as their lakes. Why are the lakes of Holland *dull?*

The chief lakes are Yesselmonde, Salt, Lange, Tjeuke.

313 How unlike (they are to) **their Belgic sires of old,** (who were) **rough . . bold.**

Belgic. Belgica of the Romans embraced a large district, bounded on the east by the Rhine, and extending westward nearly to the Seine (Sequana). It covered a part of the area now occupied by France and Holland. A tribe called the Batavi inhabited the north-eastern part south of the Rhine. The tribe north of the Rhine where part of Holland now lies, belonged to the Frisii. Hence G. might more correctly have said *Batavic* or *Frisic*.

Sires. Lat. *senior;* Fr. *seigneur* contracted into *sire*.

315 War and freedom are in the nominative absolute. It is *their Belgic sires* who are said to have had :

'War in each breast and freedom on each brow,'

not the modern Dutch, as some seem to have supposed.

316 The poet evidently alludes to the fact of the Dutch and English being descended from the same stock, and indulges a natural pride in boasting that his countrymen have so far outstripped their brothers, the Dutch.

317 Genius. What is the plural of *genius* in the sense in which it is here used?

318 Explain this line.

319 **Lawns.** Cf. *D. V.*, l. 35:
"'Sweet smiling village, loveliest of the lawn."

Arcadian pride. Arcadia, a country in the centre of the Peloponnesus. It was a mountainous region, but in the southern part there were many fruitful vales, and numerous streams. The inhabitants were chiefly devoted to pastoral pursuits, and were noted for their love of music, money, and freedom. Pan, the god of shepherds was worshipped as the tutelary deity of Arcadia, and it was here he invented the shepherd's flute. From these circumstances, at the revival of learning, Arcadia was taken by the poets as the ideal of pastoral beauty and happiness. —See Sidney's *Arcadia*.

320 **Famed Hydaspes.** The Hydaspes, now known as the Jhelum, is one of the tributaries of the Indus. Hydaspes is a corruption of its Sancrit name Vitastâ. *Famed* is a translation of the "fabulosus" of Horace, (Od. I. 22, 8). "The epithet *fabulous* refers to the strange accounts which were circulated respecting this river, its golden sands, the monsters inhabiting its waters, etc."

321 **All around**=in every direction. *All* is an adverb qualifying *around*, and *around* is an adverb qualifying *stray*.

322 **Spray.** A. S. *sprec*, a sprig; or from *sprædan*, to spread. The meaning is that birds sing on every branch.

Cf. Chaucer:
"The wood dove upon the *spray*,
He sang full loud and clear,"
and Dryden:
"The painted birds, companions of the spring,
Hopping from *spray* to *spray*, were heard to sing."

324 This line seems to mean that so far as climate and natural surroundings are concerned, everything in England is of the "mildest" and "gentlest" description; but that the possessors of the soil (the masters) are not so, being extreme in boldness, independence, and love of freedom.

Only is an adverb qualifying the phrase following.

325 **Stern** is here used as an adverb, to qualify *holds*.

326 **Great** qualifies *bosom*. Explain this line.

327 **Pride and defiance** are in the nominative absolute.

Port=bearing. Cf. Gray's *Bard*, 117:
"Her lion port, her awe-commanding face."

328 Lords of human kind. Who are meant? Pass by is the complement of *see.* See note on l. 41.

330 Explain this line.

Unfashioned. Lat. *facere,* to make, *factio,* a making; Fr. *façon.*

332 Above control is an adjunct of *true.*

Control. Old Fr. *contreroller;* Fr. *contrôler.*

333 While. Compare note on l. 109.

Peasant. Lat. *paganus,* a villager, from *pagus,* a village; Fr. *paysan.*

Scan. Lat. *scando,* to climb.

Boasts that he is justified in inquiring into these (his own) rights, *i.e.*, in discussing the public questions which affect him as the citizen of a great country.

To scan is the object of *boasts.*

334 As man. *As* is redundant. See *How to Parse,* par. 209.

335 See Cowper's *Task,* Bk. V.; also Addison's *Letter from Italy:*

"Oh Liberty, thou goddess heavenly bright,
Profuse of bliss, and pregnant with delight!"

337-8 (We would be) *too blest, indeed,* (if) *such* (charms) *were without alloy, but ills, fostered even by freedom, annoy.*

Alloy. Fr. *aloyer,* to make of the legal standard, from *aloi,* a standard; Old Fr. *alloye,* lawful, from *à la loi;* or Old Fr. *alloyer,* to unite, from Lat. *alligo,* to bind.

338 Even is an adverb qualifying the phrase *by freedom.*

Annoy. Lat. *ad* and *noxius,* hurtful; Fr. *ennuyer.*

341 Lordlings. A diminutive from lord, with the idea of contempt. Cf. hireling and underling.

344 Repelling and repelled. Both of these participles form adjuncts of the subject *minds.*

345 Ferments arise. 'Political agitations.'

Imprisoned factions roar. Factions which were grasping after supremacy in parliament, but were restrained by internal divisions and the strength of their opponents.

After the fall of Walpole, the Whigs who, since the Revolution had presented an unbroken front to the opposite party, became divided into families and cliques. In the words of Lord John Russell, this "was the age of small factions." At

THE TRAVELLER. 69

the accession of George III. the ministry in power had been formed by a coalition between the Duke of Newcastle and Mr. Pitt, and embraced also the Grenville and Bedford section of the Whigs. The King, "whose object was not merely to supplant one party, and establish another in its place; but to create a new party, faithful to himself, regarding his personal wishes, carrying out his policy, and depending on his will," soon succeeded in breaking up this ministry. This he accomplished chiefly by fomenting jealousies among them. Not long after the resignation of Pitt, Lord Bute, the King's favorite, became Premier, but the difficulties of his position soon induced him to resign. Mr. Grenville, in 1763, formed a ministry, but after two years of public discontent, and of disagreement within the Cabinet, he resigned, and the Marquis of Rockingham became First Lord of the Treasury.

346 It was during the term of the Grenville ministry that the imprisonment and prosecution of Wilkes took place. When the House of Lords voted a pamphlet from among Wilkes' papers to be blasphemous, and advised a prosecution, he fled to France. The public agitation in favor of "Wilkes and Liberty" was further strengthened by the injunctions issued by Grenville against the Press.

By **repressed ambition** is to be understood (by metonymy) Wilkes who, from France *(around her shore)*, was assisting in keeping up the popular agitation.

It is not improbable, that in the expression *imprisoned factions*, our poet was thinking of the imprisonment of Wilkes, in 1764.

347 Explain *general system*.

348 Stopped, fire. See note on l. 41.

Frenzy. Gr. φρήν, the mind; Lat. *phrenesis*, frenzy; Fr. *frénésie*.

351 By **fictitious bonds**, as opposed to *nature's ties*, is to be understood the bonds which men are compelled to make artificially when *nature's ties* can no longer keep society honest and honorable. Some men are honest as far as they are obliged by law to be. G. thinks they should be so from a sense of 'duty, love, and honor.'

354 Unknown is the complement of *weeps*.

356 Land of scholars. Mention those most distinguished in science and literature.

Nurse of arms. Who are England's greatest warriors?

357 Stems=families.

358 Wrote=written. Owing to the tendency to drop the inflection *en*, the Elizabethan authors frequently used the curtailed forms of past participles which are common in Early English: "I have spoke, forgot, writ, chid," etc.—Abbott's *Shakes. Gram.* 343.

359 Sink is in the predicate nominative after *lie*.

360 Unhonored. See note on l. 354. What kind of a proposition is this line?

363 Aspire. See note on l. 292.

364 Far from, etc. Parse *far* here. See note on l. 130.

365-6 What events in English History illustrate the poet's statement in these lines? Notice the alliteration of several of the lines of this beautiful apostrophe.

366 Rabble. Lat. *rabula*, a brawling advocate; *rabo*, to rave; Dut. *rabbelen*, to rattle.

Angry steel. What figure?

No doubt our poet, while penning this apostrophe to Freedom, had in his mind the struggle that was then going on between George III. and his parliament. Outside of the House, too, the strife was even greater than within. It was difficult to determine whether Freedom was suffering more at the hands of demagogues like Wilkes, or from the arbitrary conduct of the King. Every line of this part of the poem is fraught with pictures from the times in which it was written. Green's *History*, and May's *Constitutional History*, should be carefully consulted.

368 Fostering. A. S. *fostrian*, to foster; from *foster*, originally *fodster*, food. "When two consonants come together the first is often assimilated to the second, or the second to the first, thus *d* or *t* + *s*, will become *s*, as *gospel, foster = godspel, fodster.*"—Dr. R. Morris.

369 Changeful clime. Explain these words.

370 Notice the position of *only*. Account for it.

Them. To what does *them* refer?

372 Examine the truth of this statement.

Those who .. those that. Why so written?

Govern. Gr. $\varkappa \upsilon \beta \varepsilon \rho \nu \widehat{\omega}$, to steer, to govern; Lat. *guberno;* It. *governare;* Fr. *gouverner.* *B* changes to *p, v*, or *m*, as *purse*, O. Fr. *borse;* *have*, O. E. *habban;* *somersault*, Fr. *soubresaut*.

THE TRAVELLER.

374 To lay is the subject of *is*.

375 One order=one class, or section of the people.

376 Below=that are below it. Being abbreviated for an adjectival phrase, *below* is to be considered an adjective.

377 After blind supply *are they*.

378 Who think it freedom when a part aspires is equal to *who think the aspiring of a part, freedom*. Consequently, the real object is the noun clause, *when a part aspires*, and *it* is the preparatory object. *Freedom* is in the objective case in apposition to the clause, *when a part aspires*.

380 Except is here a preposition showing the relation between *to rise* and the noun clause, *when . . warms*. Some consider *except* a past participle, which it originally was. In that case, the noun clause, *when . . warms*, would represent the nominative absolute.

Warms. Supply the object.

381-2 Blockade the throne. Oppose the attempts of the sovereign, to make himself absolute. It is explained by the next line.

This couplet refers to the events sketched in the note on l. 345. Who were the "contending chiefs"?

Although G. tells us in l. 362 that he does not mean "to flatter kings," yet, in view of the history of the time, it must be confessed, that his sympathies seem to be in favor of kingly domination. In the preface to his *History of England*, G. says: "For my own part . . I cannot help wishing that our monarchs may still be allowed to enjoy the power of controlling the encroachments of the great at home." Cf. *V. of W.*, ch. XIX.: "It is the interest of the great to diminish kingly power as much as possible."

384 For analysis see note on l. 378.

385 Before *each*, supply *when I behold*.

Draw. See note on l. 41.

386 Cf. *V. of W.*, ch. XIX.

388 Pillaged. Supply *to be*, and see note on l. 41.

Purchase. Low Lat. *purchacia;* It. *procacciare;* Fr. *pourchasser*, to chase after, to hunt. - With Chaucer, *purchasour* meant prosecutor, and *purchas*, anything acquired by any means. See *Prologue to the Canterbury Tales*, ll. 256, 318 and 320.

391 This line forms an adjunct of the subject *I*.

Half. For parsing see note on l. 198.

Coward. Several derivations of this word have been proposed. A corruption of *cowherd*, Junius. Lat. *culum vertere*, to turn tail, Twisden. Past participle of the verb *to cower*, Tooke. Lat. *cauda*, a tail; O. Fr. *coue*, as frightened animals put their tail between their legs, Todd. It. *codards;* Fr. *couard*.

394 When . . power. This clause is adjectival to *hour*. To what does the poet appear to refer in this line?

395 After *and*, supply *when ambition*.

Wealth is the indirect object, and *to sway*, etc., is the direct.

396 Double force. Why?

397-8 Have we not seen the peasant population of England, forced to emigrate to distant countries on account of the increase of wealth (ore)? Cf. *D. V.*, 49-56.

Parse *exchanged*. See note on line 41.

Exchanged. Lat. *ex*, from, and *cambiare*, to exchange; Fr. *échanger*.

399 Before *seen*, supply *have we not*.

Have we not seen that all her triumphs only tend to hasten her own destruction?

But is an adverb qualifying the infinitive *haste*, i.e., to hasten. Ger. *hast;* O. Fr. *haste;* Fr. *hâte*.

Destruction is the object of *haste*.

400 After *tapers*, supply *hasten their destruction*.

For parsing of *like*, see note on l. 27.

401 Before *seen*, supply *have we not*. Cf. *D. V.*, 63-66.

405 *D. V.*, 275-282:

"The man of wealth and pride
Takes up a place that many poor supplied—
Space for his lake, his park's extended bounds,
Space for his horses, equipage and hounds;
The robe that wraps his limbs in silken sloth,
Has robb'd the neighboring fields of half their growth;
His seat, where solitary sports are seen,
Indignant spurns the cottage from the green."

407 Supply *have we not* before *beheld*. Cf. *D. V.*, 362-384.

Decayed. Explain this word.

409 Forced. Parse this word. See l. 41.

411 Oswego. The river is here meant. Trace its course minutely on the map. Give its other name. Cf. G.'s *Threnodia Augustalis:*

"Oswego's dreary shores shall be my grave."

THE TRAVELLER. 73

412 Niagara is here accented on the penult. It is so marked in Lippincott's *Gazetteer*.

413-22 This somewhat difficult passage is analyzed thus: *Even now, perhaps, there, the pensive exile, bending with his woe, to stop too fearful, and too faint to go, casts a long look*, forms the first principal proposition. L. 422 contains a principal proposition co-ordinate with this.

As then . . ways is a subordinate adverbial clause qualifying *casts* in l. 421. *Where . . claim* is adjectival to *ways*, as, also, is *(where) the brown . . aim*. *While . . flies* and *(while) all around . . arise*, are each adverbial to *casts*.

413 Pilgrim. Lat. *per*, through, and *ager*, a land; *peregrinus*, a foreigner; It. *pellegrino;* Fr. *pèlerin;* Cf. Dut. *pelgrim;* Ger. *pilger;* Dan. *pilgrim*.

414-6 Cf. *D. V.*, ll. 349-356:

"Those matted woods where birds forget to sing,
And silent bats in drowsy clusters cling;
Those poisonous fields with rank luxuriance crown'd,
Where the dark scorpion gathers death around;
Where at each step the stranger fears to wake
The rattling terrors of the vengeful snake;
Where crouching tigers wait their hapless prey,
And savage men more murderous still than they."

416 Indian. Explain how the aborigines of America came to be called *Indians*.

417 Giddy tempest. What figure? See note on l. 187.

418 All is an adverb, qualifying *around*.

419 Exile. Lat. *exilium* or *exsilium*, exile; *exsul*, one driven from his native land, from *ex*, out of, and *solum*, land.

420 This line was written by Dr. Johnson. "In the year 1783, he, at my request, marked with a pencil the lines which he had furnished, which are only line 420 and the concluding ten lines, except the last couplet but one. He added, 'these are all of which I can be sure.' They bear a small proportion to the whole."—Boswell's *Life of Johnson*, ch. XIX.

422 Mine, a pronoun, the possessive case of *I*, euphonic form for *my*, possessing *bosom* understood; or an adjective used substantively. See note on l. 50.

423 To find, etc., is an adjunct of *search*.

424 Only qualifies the phrase *in the mind*, and should stand immediately before it.

426 Government. See note on l. 372.

Cf. Pope's *Essay on Man*:

"For forms of government let fools contest;
Whate'er is best administer'd, is best."

429 How small that part of all, etc., (is) in every government is the principal proposition. See note on l. 420.

Cf. Macaulay's *Essay on Boswell's Life of Johnson*: "His calm and settled opinion seems to have been, that forms of government have little or no influence on the happiness of society."

431 Still = ever.

After *felicity* supply *which is*, and read, *our own felicity which is consigned to ourselves in every place*, i.e., in every country and under every form of government. Cf. Milton's *P. L.*, I. 254:

"The mind is its own place, and in itself
Can make a heaven of hell, a hell of heaven."

433 Secret. Cf. Milton's *P. L.*, I. 6:

"Sing, heavenly Muse, that on the secret top
Of Oreb."

Also Gray's *Elegy*, l. 11:

"Wandering near her secret bower."

435 Agonizing wheel.

"Breaking on the wheel was a very barbarous mode of inflicting the punishment of death, formerly in use in France and Germany, where the criminal was placed on a carriage-wheel, with his arms and legs extended along the spokes, and the wheel being turned round, the executioner fractured his limbs by successive blows with an iron bar, which were repeated till death ensued. The punishment of the wheel was abolished in France at the Revolution; in Germany it has occasionally been inflicted during the present century."—Chambers's *Encyclopædia*.

436 Luke's iron crown.

"Who was Luke, and what was his iron crown? is a question Tom Davies tells us he had often to answer; being a great resource in difficulties of that kind. 'The Doctor referred me,' he says, in a letter to the reverend Mr. Granger, who was compiling his *Biographical History* and wished to be exact, 'to a book called *Géographie Curieuse*, for an explanation of Luke's iron crown.' The explanation, besides being in itself incorrect, did not mend matters much. 'Luke' had been taken simply for the euphony of the line. He was one of two brothers Dosa who had headed a revolt against the Hungarian nobles, at the beginning of the sixteenth century; but, though both were tortured, the special horror of the red-hot crown was inflicted upon George. 'Dr. Goldsmith says,' adds Davies, 'he meant by Damiens' iron, the rack; *but I believe* the newspapers informed us that he was confined in a high tower, and actually obliged to lie upon an iron bed.'"—Forster's *Life of Goldsmith*.

Damiens' bed of steel.

"Robert F. Damiens, on January 5th, 1757, stabbed Louis XV., slightly wounding him, in his right side, when the king was entering his carriage at Versailles. His motives are not known; Damiens himself alleged that it was the conduct of the King towards the Parliament. A fearful punishment was inflicted. The hand by which he attempted the murder was burned at a slow fire; the fleshy parts of his body were then torn off by pincers; and finally he was dragged about for an hour by four strong horses, while into his numerous wounds were poured molten lead, resin, oil, and boiling wax."—Chambers's *Encyclopædia*.

437 To men . . known is an adjectival clause qualifying *axe, wheel, crown* and *bed*.

Parse *but* here.

438 All = entirely, is an adverb qualifying *our own*. For parsing of *our own*, see note on l. 30.

LIFE OF GRAY.

EMERSON, speaking of Plato, says : "Great geniuses have the shortest biographies. Their cousins can tell you nothing about them. They lived in their writings, and so their house and street life was trivial and commonplace. If you would know their tastes and complexions, the most admiring of their readers most resemble them. Plato especially has no external biography. As a good chimney burns its smoke, so a philosopher converts the value of all his fortunes into his intellectual performances." These pertinent remarks apply with singular aptness to Gray. Quiet and retiring in youth, a bookworm in his maturer years, there is comparatively little material for the biographer. A knowledge of him and his inner life is to be gleaned chiefly from the fitful bursts of feeling almost unconsciously flashing out in the few pages his genius has left us.

Thomas Gray was born in Cornhill, London, on the 26th of December, 1716. His father, Philip Gray, was a money-scrivener. Though nominally a 'respectable citizen,' and comparatively wealthy, he was a man of harsh and violent disposition. He treated his family with such brutal severity and neglect, that his wife was forced to separate from him. It was to the exertions of this excellent woman, as partner with a sister in the millinery business, that Gray owed the advantages of a learned education. The painful domestic circumstances of his youth gave him a tinge of melancholy and pensive reflection, which makes itself visible in all his writings. For the mother, to whose solicitude and self-sacrificing devotion he owed so much, he ever entertained the highest respect and always manifested a tender filial regard.

Of Gray's boyhood days almost nothing is known. At a comparatively early age, he entered Eton under the charge of Mr. Antrobus, a maternal uncle, at that time one of the assistants in the school. Here began his friendship with Horace Walpole, son of the celebrated prime minister, Sir Robert Walpole. Here, too, he formed his first acquaintance with Richard West, son of the Chancellor of Ireland. With the latter, similar tastes and congeniality of pursuits ripened into a very warm attachment which was terminated only by the untimely death of West. Bryant, a fellow-student, afterwards a voluminous writer, and secretary to Marlborough, speaks of Gray's figure as small and elegant, his manners delicate and refined, and his morals without a stain. In a public school, where not to be riotous is to be unpopular, such characteristics would win slight regard. He disliked all rough exercise, and seldom was seen in the fields. Amongst the other pupils, his shrinking nature and solitary habits passed for affectation and pride. Left to a great extent to his own fancies and meditations, he "began," as he tells us, "to take pleasure in reading Virgil for his own amusement, and not in school hours as a task." In the midst of this semi-seclusion, his unchecked life passed on until he entered Peterhouse, Cambridge, in 1734. Of his college life little more can be gathered than, that he was not a very ardent student, and that he disliked both the mode of life and the 'fashion of study.' During his residence at college, he wrote a few minor poems : *Luna Habitabilis, Verses on the Marriage of the Prince of Wales,* a *Sapphic Ode to West,* and some translations.

In 1739, at the request of Horace Walpole, Gray accompanied him in his travels abroad, and, from his letters to West and his own family, we have a tolerably accurate account of his pursuits. He wrote a minute description of everything he saw on his tour from Rome to Naples. His impressions are given like sun-pictures, with the glowing truthfulness of life. He not only sketched in an inimitable manner the customs and manners of the people, but gave evidence of a fine taste and extensive learning, by his critical observations on arts and antiquities. At Florence, he made a collection of music chiefly embracing the works of the old Italian masters. At Reggio, the companions quarrelled and parted. The cause of the disagreement has not been ascertained. About three years afterwards, by the intervention of a lady, a partial reconciliation was effected, and Walpole redeemed his youthful error by a life-long admiration and respect for his friend. From Reggio, Gray proceeded to Venice, thence he travelled homewards by nearly the same route as he had come to Italy, revisiting the monastery of Grande Chartreuse situated near Grenoble in France. Here he wrote some beautiful verses in the monastery album. A letter to his mother gives in prose the spirit of these lines. "The enormous precipices, the frowning cliffs, the overhanging woods of beech and fir, and the torrents descending with the crash of thunder," combined with the solemn associations of the scene to kindle his imagination and awaken his muse. After an absence of about two years and a half, he arrived in England in September 1741. Within two months after his return his father died. The poet's mother, husbanding her remaining property, sought a home with a widowed sister at Stoke, near Windsor. Gray himself retraced his steps to Cambridge and took his Bachelor's degree in Civil Law, although his limited fortune would not permit him to finish this, his intended course. Here he spent the remainder of his uneventful life, with the exception of nearly three years' residence in London. He became a sort of literary hermit, whose chief pleasure seemed to consist in continually poring over books.

Shortly after going to Cambridge he began his tragedy of *Agrippina*, and submitted the first portion of it to his friend, West, who objected amongst other things to the antiquated style in which it was written. Although Gray warmly defended the style he never completed the tragedy.

During the early part of this summer (1742), he wrote his *Ode to Spring*, and sent it to the same critic, but it was returned unopened; his beloved friend having died of consumption before the poem reached its destination. Gray had other warm friends, but none that could fill the place of West. Years afterwards, we are assured, he scarcely ever mentioned his name without a sigh. The *Ode to Spring*, a short poem of five stanzas, exhibits in a striking manner Gray's admiration of the beautiful in nature, his acute observation, and his accurate taste; although it is overcast by that shadow of melancholy, which seemed to color every word and act of the author's life. Even Dr. Johnson, whose coarse and unjust criticism exhibits his bitter dislike for Gray, was forced to admit that this Ode "has something poetical both in the language and in the thought."

In the autumn of this year he wrote his *Ode on a distant prospect of Eton College*, and his *Hymn to Adversity*. In the former he, with true poetic fervor, gives a comprehensive description of the surrounding scenery, and in happy terms depicts the school-boy's sports and joys; but even here, on this scene of pleasing memories, the poet's uncontrollable melancholy breaks out. No glimmer of sunshine is to brighten the life of these careless youths, but "seized by black Misfortune's baleful train, these shall the fury Passions tear." The rapid sketch of the inevitable evils that are to befall man, is given with much power, but it is unfortunately marred by a sombre gloom which was doubtless deepened by the poet's sorrow over the recent death of West. Though the *Ode to Adversity* is somewhat tinged with the poet's 'tendency' it is still imposing and beautiful. Johnson says, "of this piece, at once poetical and rational, I will not by slight objections violate the dignity."

In 1744, he consented to write a poem for Walpole *On the death of a favorite Cat*. This playful and elegant poem is spoiled to a great extent by a want of harmony in the images.

During the year 1747, he became acquainted with Mr. Mason, then a scholar of St. John's College. To Mason we are indebted for many of the particulars of Gray's life. After the death of the poet, he collected his letters, sketched his life, and edited his poems. About this time, Gray began his poem, *On the Alliance of Education and Government*, but completed only about a hundred lines. Mason thinks he dropped it on finding his best thoughts forestalled by Montesquieu. Gray himself said 'he could not,' on account of the great labor. The few lines given us are, however, excellent, brilliant, and pointed. Dr. Warton said that this poem would have equalled Pope's *Essay on Man*, if the author had finished it.

In the year 1750, his *Elegy in a Country Church-yard* received the last corrections and was published by Dodsley. Shortly after this time, he was induced to write *The Long Story*, in return for hospitality shown him by Lady Cobham, at the Stoke Manor House. Throughout this poem there is a studied attempt at humor which ill becomes Gray. The author, conscious of its defects, omitted it from his collected works.

In March 1753, he lost the mother whom he had so long and affectionately loved. Over her remains he placed an inscription which strongly expresses his respect and sorrow. In one expression, "Here sleep the remains of Dorothy Gray, the tender mother of many children, one of whom alone had the misfortune to survive her," there is prominently indicated the deep-seated melancholy so characteristic of his nature.

The year 1756 was marked by one of the few changes of his uneventful life. His residence at Peterhouse had not been free from annoyances His rooms were on the middle floor, the adjoining apartments being occupied by riotous undergraduates. Irritated beyond endurance by repeated offensive acts, he complained to the authorities. Little attention being paid to his remonstrance, he became displeased and removed to Pembroke Hall, which, indeed, afforded him a calm and pleasant retreat, but which at the same time served to shut him more and more out from the world and thus to deepen the gloom at his heart.

In 1757, he published *The Progress of Poesy* and *The Bard*. Walpole in one of his letters writes : " I send you two copies of a very honorable opening of my press—two amazing odes of Mr. Gray. They are Greek, they are Pindaric, they are sublime, consequently, I fear, a little obscure ; the second particularly, by the confinement of the measure and the nature of prophetic vision, is mysterious. I could not persuade him to add more notes." Both these poems at first met with opposition rather than favor. The great objection to them was their obscurity. So much was this felt that two parodies, entitled *Odes to*

Obscurity and Oblivion, were published and met with considerable sale. Gray was afterwards unwillingly compelled to add explanatory notes. Both poems exhibit great artistic finish and a fine discrimination. The former traces the progress of Poesy through her old classic regions, and, finally, brings her after these wanderings to the home she at last found in England. Particular reference is made with appropriate grace and tenderness to Shakespeare in his familiarity with Nature in her power and beauty. The picture given of Milton is none the less distinguished by characteristic elevation and grandeur. The *Bard* is the more popular of the two. "It is certainly not superior in poetical merit, but it is infinitely more dramatic, has more fire and passion, and what may not have weighed a little in procuring its general acceptance, it deals with the striking events and epochs of our national history." It might be well to notice Johnson's severe judgment: "My process has now brought me to the *wonderful* 'Wonder of Wonders,' the two sister Odes, by which, though either vulgar ignorance or common sense at first universally rejected them, many have been since persuaded to think themselves delighted. I am one of those that are willing to be pleased, and would therefore gladly find the meaning of the first stanza of *The Progress of Poetry*. These odes are marked by glittering accumulations of ungraceful ornaments; they strike rather than please; the images are magnified by affectation; the language is labored into harshness. His art and his struggle are too visible, and there is too little appearance of ease and nature." Mr. Mathias, an able and less prejudiced critic, writes: "Antecedent to the *Progress of Poesy* and the *Bard*, no such lyrics had appeared. There is not an ode in the English language constructed like these two compositions, with such power, such majesty, and such sweetness; with such appropriate pauses, and just cadences; with such regulated measure of the verse; with such master principles of lyric art displayed and exemplified, and at the same time with such concealment of the difficulty, which is lost by the softness and uninterrupted fluency of the lines in each stanza; with such a musical magic, that every verse of it in succession dwells on the ear, and harmonizes with that which is gone before."

In this year Cibber died at an advanced age, after holding the Laureateship for twenty years; and the honor was now offered to Gray, with the privilege of holding it as a mere sinecure. This offer he, however, respectfully declined. The British Museum being opened in 1759 to the public, Gray went to London, and spent nearly three years in reading and transcribing from the manuscripts there collected. His studies whilst in London were directed mainly to historical subjects. In 1762 by the advice of his friends, Gray applied to Lord Bute for the Professorship of Modern History, which had just become vacant. His application was unsuccessful. In the summer of 1765, he took a journey to Scotland, both to improve his health and to gratify his curiosity. He gives a graphic description of these tours in letters to his friends. "His account of his travels," says Johnson, "is, so far as it extends, curious and elegant. From his comprehension, which was ample, his curiosity extended to all the works of art, the appearances of nature and all the monuments of past events." His tour afforded him a great deal of pleasure. He here made the acquaintance of Dr. Beattie, the author of *The Minstrel*, and emphatically recommended to him the study of the writings of Dryden. He told him, that if there was any excellence in his own numbers, he had learnt it wholly from that great poet;

and pressed him with earnestness to study this author, as his choice of words and versification are singularly happy and harmonious.

In 1768, the Professorship of Modern History again became vacant, and the Duke of Grafton, then in power, bestowed it on Gray. The Duke was shortly after elected to the Chancellorship of the University, and Gray returned the favor he had received by writing his *Installation Ode*. Of these stanzas, the poet himself had a poor opinion. In writing to Dr. Beattie, he said : "I do not think them worth sending you because they are by nature doomed to live but a single day." Yet Mitford sees, "throughout the whole, an almost magical splendor of coloring, a fine combination of beautiful images, appropriate words, and exquisitely regulated verse."

Ill health made another journey necessary, and he visited (1769) Cumberland and Westmoreland. During his tour, he regularly sent a journal of his travels to his old friend, Dr. Wharton. This has been printed. It is written with great simplicity, and abounds in lively and picturesque description. "He that reads his *Epistolary Narrative*," says Dr. Johnson, "wishes that to travel and tell his travels, had been more of his employment."

After this, his health rapidly declined. His mind was oppressed with gloom, and he constantly fretted himself about unperformed duties in connection with his chair, not one lecture having been delivered during his tenure of office. On the 24th of July 1771, while at dinner in the College Hall, he was seized with an attack of gout in the stomach, which, in spite of the best medical advice, proved fatal on the 30th. His remains were, at his own request, interred at Stoke-Pogis near Slough, Buckinghamshire, in the beautiful church-yard that is supposed to have furnished the scene of his *Elegy*.

In the preceding outline, brief reference has been made to the main features of Gray's character and abilities. The same tendency to reserve and isolation, which displayed itself so prominently in youth, gained power as years passed by. The timid, sad, delicate boy became the shrinking, melancholy, unhealthy man. Placed above want by an income of nearly £700, and having no definite object in life, he allowed his genius and his energies to slumber. He read and studied incessantly, but produced comparatively little from the vast stores of knowledge thus acquired. His thirst for information led him into every department of literature. Now, we have him carefully reading, annotating, or translating some ancient author; again, absorbed in some branch of history: now, an antiquarian; again, a geographer: now, exhibiting an extensive knowledge of criticism, metaphysics, morals, politics; again, showing a refined taste in painting and music: now, making nice distinctions between the different styles of architecture, or tracing genealogies by his knowledge of heraldry; again, making additions to the Natural History of Linnæus, or to some work on botany: now, buried in a French novel; again, delighting himself in translating Scandinavian or Celtic legends. Of English poetry, Gray was a critical and profound student. Goldsmith showed discernment in tracing to Spenser the compound epithets and the solemn numbers of Gray, who never sat down to write verses without reading him for a considerable time. His admiration for Dryden has already been referred to. Pope, he commended for his 'perfection of good sense.' To Milton he rendered a constantly increasing homage. Of contemporary poets he was not always a patient or a generous judge. Akenside, he turned over rather than read; Thomson he slighted; Collins he misunderstood; Beattie satisfied him less than Goldsmith, whose restless vanity might have been calmed, if he could have seen Gray listening with unbroken interest to the reading of the *Deserted Village*, and exclaiming at the end, "That man is a poet!"

One might imagine that such an extensive course of reading would necessarily induce superficiality and weakness of mental power. Such, however, was not the result in the case of Gray. He was always able to enter into an animated and exhaustive discussion on any of his favorite subjects. With the exception of mathematics, which he detested, he had an extensive acquaintance with all branches of knowledge, and was esteemed the most accomplished scholar of his time. In extensive erudition, Milton is the only English poet that can be compared with him. Milton looking beyond self and actuated by a diviner impulse, devoted his powers to the good of his fellow-beings. Gray, a recluse indifferent to the claims of society, withdrew from the "madding crowd's ignoble strife," and, wedded to his books and Pembroke Hall, permitted "grim-visaged comfortless Despair" to seize upon and destroy the best promptings of his heart.

A serious effect, and one to be deeply regretted, which Gray's varied and extensive range of study had upon himself, was to limit his power of production. His taste became extremely fastidious. Quick in detecting blemishes, he was not slow to censure them in others. Actuated by a desire for critical accuracy, he could not permit anything to flow from his pen that was either crude or imperfectly finished. It is only at extended intervals, during the long period of twenty-nine years, that his spirit breaks through the artificial restraints imposed upon it, and shows bright gleams of inspiration. In this and other respects, he differs very largely from

Goldsmith. Gray wrote only for his own pleasure, or for that of his immediate friends, and laboriously as well as unsparingly corrected and modified his verses till they suited his critical taste. Goldsmith driven by want wrote rapidly, ceaselessly, and often carelessly. Gray touches our hearts and enlists our sympathies—his highest art concealed by art. Goldsmith carries us with him, using no art, but speaking from a soul filled to overflowing with Nature's generous impulses. Gray's extensive learning and vivid imagination are apparent in every line. Goldsmith presents pictures from observation rather than from fancy, and delights us most when sketching some real scene or character. Gray generally convinces by appealing directly to the reason. Goldsmith reaches our judgment through our feelings. Gray was reserved, distant, fastidious, of careful and retired habits, methodical in his pursuits, handsome and neat in person. Goldsmith, on the contrary, was genial, affable, easy, improvident, inconstant, negligent in his attire and unprepossessing in appearance. Yet, widely as they differed, they resembled each other in their extreme sensibility to praise or censure. But while Gray seldom forgot an injury, Goldsmith forgave before pardon was asked ; and, while the one neither sought nor avoided praise, the good-will of the other could at any time be won by a commendation of himself or his productions.

ELEGY WRITTEN IN A COUNTRY CHURCH-YARD.

INTRODUCTION.

THE *Elegy*, begun in 1742, was not finished till the year 1750. For some time after it was written, Gray permitted it to circulate amongst his friends, in manuscript. At last, through the carelessness of Walpole—or it may have been a friendly wish of his to see it universally admired, as he felt it would be—a copy fell into the hands of the editor of the *Magazine of Magazines*, who forthwith informed the poet of his intention to publish it. Gray at once wrote to Walpole : " I have but one bad way left to escape the honor they would inflict upon me : and therefore am obliged to desire you would make Dodsley print it immediately (which may be done in less than a week's time) from your copy, but without my name, in what form is most convenient for him, but on his best paper and character ; he must correct the press himself, and print it without any interval between the stanzas, because the sense is in some places continued beyond them, and the title must be—*Elegy written in a Country Church-yard.* If he would add a line or two to say it came into his hands by accident, I should like it better." Walpole did as he was requested, and, in his advertisement, informed the reader, that the publication was entirely due to an unavoidable accident. But Dodsley was too late. It appeared in the *Magazine* in February 1751, a few days before Dodsley's edition, which was published in quarto, price sixpence, with *An Elegy wrote in a Country Church-yard* for its title, and the title-page duly adorned with cross bones, skulls, and hour-glasses. The original manuscript is still in existence. It consists of the four sides of a doubled half-sheet of yellow foolscap, and is written in a neat, legible hand. Curious and interesting differences exist between the first draft and the printed copy.

The poem became so popular that the rapidity of its sale surprised even the poet himself, who modestly attributed its success to the subject, saying that its reception would have been as favorable if it had appeared in prose. It went through four editions in two months, and no fewer than twelve were called for within two years. Ever since its publication, its popularity has been steadily increasing. At the present time, it is safe to say, that there is no poem so well known or so widely read. "One peculiar and remarkable tribute to the merit of the *Elegy*," says Professor Henry Reed, "is to be noticed in the great number of translations which have been made of it into various languages, both of ancient and modern Europe. It is the same kind of tribute which has been rendered to *Robinson Crusoe* and to *The Pilgrim's Progress*, and is proof of the same universality of interest, transcending the limits of language and race. To no poem in the English language has the same kind of homage been paid so abundantly." The same writer furnishes an incomplete list of the translations to which he refers. These include one in Hebrew, seven in Greek, twelve in Latin, thirteen in Italian, fifteen in French, six in German, and one in Portuguese. We have also the following favorable testimony from Dr. Johnson, all the more valuable, as it forms so strong a contrast to his general estimate of

INTRODUCTION.

Gray's productions: "In the character of the *Elegy*, I rejoice to concur with the common reader. 'The churchyard' abounds with images which find a mirror in every mind, and with sentiments to which every bosom returns an echo. Had Gray written often thus, it had been vain to blame, and useless to praise him." Byron thus expresses his high esteem of the *Elegy:* "Had Gray written nothing but his *Elegy*, high as he stands, I am not sure that he would not stand higher; it is the cornerstone of his glory."

The reason of the wide-spread popularity of this poem, would seem to lie in the fact, that it expresses, in an easy, natural way, feelings and emotions that, time after time, have risen in every breast. Its very naturalness and simplicity win the heart and enlist the sympathies. Speculations on the strange problems of life and death, will at times force themselves upon the mind, but, on no occasion more than when in the presence of the dead. Need it be then wondered at, that an almost irresistible fascination takes possession of the reader when engaged in perusing what, to him, is largely a reflex of his own serious meditations?

By a few facile strokes of the pen, in his inimitable manner, the poet draws the deepening shades of twilight in upon us, and, amid the general hush of Nature, presents us with a view of the church-yard and its 'rugged elms.' In that lone spot, the poet's meditations carry him back to the 'toils' and 'homely joys' of the 'rude forefathers.' The imposing 'tomb,' the 'storied urn,' the 'animated bust' impress neither him nor us so deeply as the 'frail memorial with shapeless sculpture deck'd.' Fancy awakened by these suggestive surroundings, in pensive mood, moralizes on the possibilities and probabilities of the lives of those interred beneath these 'mouldering heaps.' Forbidden by their lot to attain to eminence and power, still amongst them may there not have been many a mind capable of wielding a controlling influence over the destinies of our race. At each successive reading, we linger with delight, over those expressive and affecting lines which show the fearfulness of the soul when passing alone into the "dark unknown." Almost unconsciously we are led by the poet into his own inner life. Identifying himself with those amongst whose tombs he meditates, he allows his mind to recall his own pursuits, and finally to anticipate the closing scenes in his own earthly career. At the poet's bidding we read the Epitaph—an epitaph penned by a gentle yet faithful hand, and rise from our reveries with feelings solemnized and emotions subdued

ELEGY WRITTEN IN A COUNTRY CHURCH-YARD.

THE curfew tolls the knell of parting day,
    The lowing herd wind slowly o'er the lea,
The ploughman homeward plods his weary way,
    And leaves the world to darkness and to me.

Now fades the glimmering landscape on the sight,   5
    And all the air a solemn stillness holds,
Save where the beetle wheels his droning flight,
    And drowsy tinklings lull the distant folds;

Save that, from yonder ivy-mantled tower,
    The moping owl does to the moon complain   10
Of such as, wandering near her secret bower,
    Molest her ancient solitary reign.

Beneath those rugged elms, that yew-tree's shade,
    Where heaves the turf in many a mould'ring heap,
Each in his narrow cell forever laid,   15
    The rude forefathers of the hamlet sleep.

The breezy call of incense-breathing morn,
    The swallow twittering from the straw-built shed,
The cock's shrill clarion, or the echoing horn,
    No more shall rouse them from their lowly bed.   20

For them no more the blazing hearth shall burn,
  Or busy housewife ply her evening care ;
No children run to lisp their sire's return,
  Or climb his knees the envied kiss to share.

Oft did the harvest to their sickle yield,   25
  Their furrow oft the stubborn glebe has broke ;
How jocund did they drive their team afield !
  How bow'd the woods beneath their sturdy stroke !

Let not Ambition mock their useful toil,
  Their homely joys, and destiny obscure ;   30
Nor Grandeur hear with a disdainful smile
  The short and simple annals of the poor.

The boast of heraldry, the pomp of power,
  And all that beauty, all that wealth e'er gave,
Await alike th' inevitable hour :   35
  The paths of glory lead but to the grave.

Nor you, ye proud, impute to these the fault,
  If Memory o'er their tomb no trophies raise,
Where, through the long-drawn aisle and fretted vault,
  The pealing anthem swells the note of praise.   40

Can storied urn or animated bust
  Back to its mansion call the fleeting breath ?
Cán Honor's voice provoke the silent dust,
  Or Flattery soothe the dull cold ear of Death ?

Perhaps in this neglected spot is laid 45
  Some heart once pregnant with celestial fire;
Hands, that the rod of empire might have sway'd,
  Or wak'd to ecstasy the living lyre:

But Knowledge to their eyes her ample page,
  Rich with the spoils of time, did ne'er unroll; 50
Chill Penury repress'd their noble rage,
  And froze the genial current of the soul.

Full many a gem of purest ray serene
  The dark unfathom'd caves of ocean bear;
Full many a flower is born to blush unseen, 55
  And waste its sweetness on the desert air.

Some village Hampden, that with dauntless breast
  The little tyrant of his fields withstood;
Some mute inglorious Milton here may rest,
  Some Cromwell, guiltless of his country's blood. 60

Th' applause of list'ning senates to command,
  The threats of pain and ruin to despise,
To scatter plenty o'er a smiling land,
  And read their history in a nation's eyes,

Their lot forbade: nor circumscrib'd alone 65
  Their growing virtues, but their crimes confin'd;
Forbade to wade through slaughter to a throne,
  And shut the gates of mercy on mankind;

The struggling pangs of conscious truth to hide,
To quench the blushes of ingenuous shame, 70
Or heap the shrine of Luxury and Pride
With incense kindled at the Muse's flame.

Far from the madding crowd's ignoble strife,
Their sober wishes never learn'd to stray,
Along the cool sequester'd vale of life 75
They kept the noiseless tenor of their way.

Yet ev'n these bones from insult to protect,
Some frail memorial still erected nigh,
With uncouth rhymes and shapeless sculpture deck'd,
Implores the passing tribute of a sigh. 80

Their name, their years, spelt by th' unletter'd Muse,
The place of fame and elegy supply;
And many a holy text around she strews,
That teach the rustic moralist to die.

For who, to dumb Forgetfulness a prey, 85
This pleasing anxious being e'er resign'd,
Left the warm precincts of the cheerful day,
Nor cast one longing ling'ring look behind?

On some fond breast the parting soul relies,
Some pious drops the closing eye requires; 90
Ev'n from the tomb the voice of Nature cries,
Ev'n in our ashes live their wonted fires.

For thee, who, mindful of th' unhonor'd dead,
  Dost in these lines their artless tale relate ;
If chance, by lonely Contemplation led, 95
  Some kindred spirit shall inquire thy fate,

Haply some hoary-headed swain may say,
  " Oft have we seen him at the peep of dawn
Brushing with hasty steps the dews away,
  To meet the sun upon the upland lawn. 100

" There at the foot of yonder nodding beech,
  That wreathes its old fantastic roots so high,
His listless length at noontide would he stretch,
  And pore upon the brook that babbles by.

" Hard by yon wood, now smiling as in scorn, 105
  Mutt'ring his wayward fancies he would rove ;
Now drooping, woeful-wan, like one forlorn,
  Or craz'd with care, or cross'd in hopeless love.

" One morn I miss'd him on the 'custom'd hill,
  Along the heath, and near his fav'rite tree ; 110
Another came ; nor yet beside the rill, -
  Nor up the lawn, nor at the wood was he ;

" The next, with dirges due, in sad array,
  Slow through the church-way path we saw him borne.
Approach and read (for thou canst read) the lay 115
  Grav'd on the stone beneath yon aged thorn."

A 7

GRAY'S ELEGY.

THE EPITAPH.

Here rests his head upon the lap of Earth
A youth to Fortune and to Fame unknown;
Fair Science frown'd not on his humble birth,
And Melancholy mark'd him for her own.   120

Large was his bounty, and his soul sincere,
Heav'n did a recompense as largely send:
He gave to Mis'ry all he had, a tear;
He gain'd from Heav'n ('twas all he wish'd) a friend.

No farther seek his merits to disclose,   125
Or draw his frailties from their dread abode,
(There they alike in trembling hope repose)
The bosom of his Father and his God.

NOTES.

THE ELEGY.

EPITOME.

The poem opens with a description of the church-yard and its surroundings as they appear in the mellow shades of twilight. The grassy mounds of the grave-yard lead the poet to meditate on the life and fate of its humble occupants. He recounts their cares, their labors and their joys, and then calls upon the great of the earth not to despise the simple story of the poor, bidding them remember that death comes alike to all, and that their posthumous honors can as little recall them to life, as these 'neglected' graves can reanimate the poor. He continues to reflect how circumstances alone prevented them from attaining the positions and wielding the influence for which their natural abilities fitted them; how, likewise, their lot prevented them from committing the crimes and follies of those in higher spheres of life. But even they have not passed away unremembered, for these 'frail memorials' perpetuate their memory while instructing future generations. This reminds the poet of the universal desire to be remembered after death, and, as he thinks upon it, he feels rising in his own breast the same anxious craving for like immortality. His musings lead him to identify his own lot with that of the lowly sleepers, and he imagines he hears a "hoary-headed swain" narrating the story of his own life to some meditative inquirer, who is directed to read his epitaph—

"Graved on the stone beneath yon aged thorn."

With this epitaph the poem closes.

Several places claim the honor of having been the scene of the *Elegy*. According to some authorities, Granchester, a parish at a short distance from Cambridge University, is the spot, since Gray took his daily walk thither; the great bell of St. Mary's would answer to the 'curfew' of the first stanza. A similar claim is made for Madingley, about three miles and a half from Cambridge. Both the above mentioned spots answer the description so far as the church-yard is concerned, but scarcely any further. One writer has suggested a parish, called Burnham Beeches in Buckinghamshire, for the simple reason that Gray once wrote a description of the place to Walpole, and casually mentioned the existence of certain "beeches" at the foot of which he would "squat," and "there grow to the trunk a whole morning."

Of the various places suggested, the claims of Stoke-Pogis near Windsor, would appear to be the best. In visiting the Stoke Manor House, which he did very frequently, Gray had to pass and repass this church-yard. Bryant, one of Gray's fellow-students at Eton, says on this point: "In some of the stanzas towards the end, he has given a description of the lawn, heath, beeches and springs of water, near which he with his mother resided. The nature of the country is too precisely pointed out to be mistaken." In that church-yard his mother was buried, and there, at his own request, his remains were afterwards laid beside hers.

---

1 Curfew. Fr. *couvre-feu*, cover fire, "a bell rung in England in the Norman period, at eight o'clock every night, to warn the people to cover up their fires and retire to rest. Something of the same kind, probably, existed in Anglo-Saxon times, but the name just mentioned was, of course, introduced by the Normans, and we have no express allusion to the practice in England before the Anglo-Norman period. Hence has arisen the erroneous notion that the *couvre-feu* bell was instituted by William the Conqueror as an instrument of tyranny."—Chambers's *Book of Days*, Vol. II. 333.

The ringing of this bell was instituted mainly for two reasons; first, for protection from fire, most of the houses being wooden and covered with thatch; secondly, as a means of reducing as far as possible the plundering, robbery and murder so prevalent after dark, at that period, by making it criminal for any one to be found out-of-doors after the hour of eight. The practice of ringing this bell was common in France, Italy and Spain, and probably in all parts of continental Europe. The curfew-bell is still rung in many parts of England, though its original significance is lost. See *Tempest*, V., i. 40; *Lear*, III., iv. 40; *Il Penseroso*, l. 74; *Romeo and Juliet*, IV., iv. 4.

Tolls. Dr. Warton would spoil the tranquil simplicity of

this line, by introducing a note of exclamation after *tolls*. But such affectation of solemnity and surprise is nowhere to be found in our author.

Mitford objects to the word "tolls," saying the curfew was rung, not tolled. But in reference to the manner, cf. *Il Pens.*:

"Swinging slow with sullen roar."

Dante's *Purgat.*, 8, translated by Longfellow:

"From far away a bell
That seemeth to deplore the dying day."

Dryden, *Prol. to Troilus and Cressida*:

"That tolls the knell for their departed sense."

Parting=departing. Cf. Milton, *Hymn on Nat.*, l. 186; Shakes., *Cor.*, V. 6; *H. IV.*, I. i. 101; Goldsmith, *D. V.*, l. 171; Byron, *Childe Harold*, Canto IV., sta. 29; Scott, *Marmion*, III., xiii.

Cf. *D. V.*, l. 363:

"Good Heaven! what sorrows gloom'd that parting day."

2 Wind, and not *winds*, is the reading of Gray's corrected MS., and of all the early editions. *Winds* appears in the unauthorized edition of 1751. Rolfe says: "The poet does not refer to the herd as an aggregate, but to the animals that compose it. He sees not *it* but *them* on their winding way. The ordinary reading mars both the meaning and the melody of the line." Other editions read "herds wind."

3 This line will afford a good exercise for transposition. A critic says of it: "We have made twenty different versions preserving the rhythm, the general sentiment and the rhyming word. Any one of these variations might be, not inappropriately, substituted for the original reading."

Cf. Burns' *Cotter's Sat. Night:*

"And weary, o'er the moor, his course does hameward bend."

Spenser, *F. Q.*, VI., 7, 39:

"And now she was upon the weary way."

Plods. How appropriately this word expresses the slow, dragging walk of the toil-worn laborer may be seen by substituting any one of its synonyms.

Cf. *All's well that ends well*, III., iv. 5:

"Ambitious love hath so in me offended,
That barefoot plod I the cold ground upon."

THE ELEGY.

Weary way. "The adverbial objective." See *How to Parse*, par. 131. *Plods* is intransitive.

5 Now fades, etc. This sta. seems to bring twilight before the reader's mind. It is graphic, and "purely appropriate, without being for an instant tame or undignified."
Cf. Milton :
"Now is the pleasant time,
The cool, the silent, save where silence yields
To the night-warbling bird, that now awake,
Tunes sweetest his love-labor'd song."
Milton :
"Now came still evening on, and twilight gray
Had in her sober livery all things clad;
Silence accompany'd."

Glimmering. A diminutive of *gleam*. Dut. *glimmen;* Ger. *glimmen* or *glimmern*.

Cf. Shakes.:
"The west yet *glimmers* with some streaks of day."

Landscape. By this word the poet may mean the image of the landscape formed on the organs of vision *(on the sight)*, which, as evening closes down, becomes more and more indistinct.

6 All, another reading is *now*.

Air is the objective after *holds*.

Solemn. Lat. *sollennis*, from *sollus*, complete, and *annus*, a year; prop., that 'takes place every year,' and as some religious festivals were held at the end of the year, it came to have the meaning of religious, solemn.

Holds=pervades.

7 Save, like 'except,' (see *Traveller*, l. 380) is now generally parsed as a preposition. Originally, it would seem that both words were passive participles, the noun in connection with them being in the nominative absolute. Angus, in his *Handbook*, sec. 521, says these words were originally imperatives.

See *How to Parse*, par. 471 ; *Shakes. Gram.*, par. 118.

Save where the beetle, etc. Cf. Collins, *Ode to Evening:*
"Now air is hush'd, save where the weak-eyed bat
With short shrill shriek flits by on leathern wing,
Or where the beetle winds
His small but sullen horn."

THE ELEGY.

Macbeth, III. 2:

"Ere the bat hath flown
His cloister'd flight; ere to black Hecate's summons,
The shard-borne beetle, with his drowsy hums,
Hath rung night's yawning peal."

Droning, giving a dull, buzzing sound. Dryden:

"The cymbal's droning sound."

Droning flight and **drowsy tinklings.** What figure? See note on l. 187 of the *Traveller*.

8 **Drowsy**=lulling, producing a sleepy effect. Cf. *Othello*, III. 3, "Drowsy syrups"; Spenser, "Drowsy couch"; Addison, "Drowsy murmurs."

Tinklings, the same word as *tingle*, by the change of *g* into *k*. Lat. *tinnio;* Fr. *tinter*. Gray spelt it *tinkleings*.

Folds, by metonymy for the flocks.

9 **Save,** a preposition, the clause following being the object. The construction is similar to that in l. 7.

That. In such constructions *that* was originally a demonstrative pronoun, meaning *that fact* or *circumstance*, the clause following being in apposition. *That* may now be regarded as a mere introductory word.

Yonder. What part of speech?

Mantled. Lat. *mantelum* or *mantellum*, a cloak; Fr. *manteau;* S. *mæntel;* Dut., Ger., Dan., Swed., *mantel*.

Tower. A. S. *tor, torr, tur*, a rock, a peak, a tower; Dut. *toren;* Ger. *thurm;* Ir. and Gael. *tor, tur;* Gr. τύρσις, τίρρις; Lat. *turris;* Fr. *tour*.

Ivy-mantled tower. By this is meant the old church at Stoke-Pogis, thickly overgrown with ivy.

10 **Moping.** Dut. *moppen*, to pout. Cf. Milton, *P. L.*, XI. 485: "Moping melancholy."

The moping owl. Cf. Ovid, *Met.*, V. 550:

"Ignavus bubo, dirum mortalibus omen."

Thomson, *Winter*, l. 114:

"Assiduous in his bower the wailing owl
Plies his sad song."

Complain. Lat. *con*, intensive, and *plangere*, to beat the breast in token of grief; Fr. *complainte*.

11 **As** does duty for a relative pronoun.

Wandering. A. S. *wandrian*, from *wendan*, to go; Ger. *wandern;* Lat. *vadere*, to go, to walk.

Near, a preposition.

Secret. See note on l. 433 of the *Traveller.*

Bower. A. S. *bur*, a cottage, a chamber; W. *bwr*, an inclosure; Ger. *bauer.* A place of retirement, a shelter. Cf. Milton:

"Hand in hand alone they passed
On to their blissful bower."

12 Molest, etc. A MS. variation of this line is: "Molest and pry into her ancient reign."

Molest. Lat. *molestus* from *moles*, a mass; Fr. *molester.*

Reign, here equal to Lat. *regnum*, kingdom, the place reigned over; cf. Virgil, *Georgics*, III. 476: "desertaque regna pastorum."

Pope:

"The wrath which hurl'd to Pluto's gloomy reign
The souls of mighty chiefs untimely slain."

Explain allusion.

13 Beneath .. sleep. After the charming description in the preceding stas., we have now the picture of the specific subject of the poem entered into more minutely.

"In Christian countries, if the remains of the saint to whom a church was dedicated could be obtained, they were buried near the altar in the choir. Hence arose the desire to be buried within the church in order to be near these relics, and consequently the bodies of men eminent for their piety or high in rank, came to be buried in churches."—Chambers's *Encyclopædia.*

The extension of this practice was the origin of church-yards. The poor especially and many others, unable to secure any portion of the church for the remains of their friends, contented themselves with depositing them in the ground immediately surrounding the church.

Rugged. O. Fr. *rugueux;* Sw. *ruggig;* akin to rough.

Elms. Ger. *ulme;* Lat. *ulmus.*

Cf. Milton, *Arcades:*

"Under the shady roof
Of branching elms star-proof."

Tennyson, *The Princess:*

"The moan of doves in immemorial elms."

THE ELEGY.

Yew tree. A. S. *iw;* Mid. Lat. *ivus;* Fr. *if.*
These 'rugged elms' and 'yew-trees' are still to be seen, in the church-yard at Stoke-Pogis.

14 Where heaves, etc., where the turf rises in mounds above the graves. This is an adverbial clause qualifying the phrases, *beneath* . . *elms* and *beneath* . . *shade.*

Turf. Cf. Byron, *Marco Bozzaris:*

"Green be the turf above thee
Friend of my better days."

Beattie, *The Minstrel:*

"Mine be the breezy hill that skirts the down;
Where a green grassy turf is all I crave."

Many a. See note on the *Traveller*, l. 198.

15 Each. Nominative in apposition to *forefathers.* See note on l. 89 of the *Traveller.*

16 The rude . . sleep. Sir Egerton Brydges says: "I know not what there is of spell in this simple line, but no frequency of repetition can exhaust its touching charm."

Rude, unpolished, uneducated; not in its usual bad sense. Cf. Spenser: "The rude Irish books."

Shaks., *Othello*, I. 3:

"Rude am I in my speech,
And little bless'd with the soft phrase of peace."

Cf. *Traveller*, l. 3: "Rude Carinthian boor."

Hamlet. A. S. *ham,* home, and *let* diminutive; Nor. Fr. *hamelle.* Cf. Milton:

"Sometimes with secure delight
The upland hamlets will invite."

Beattie, *The Minstrel:*

"At the close of the day, when the hamlet is still
And mortals the sweets of forgetfulness prove."

17 The breezy . . bed.

"This is one of the most striking stanzas in Gray's *Elegy*, which owes much of its celebrity to the concordance of numbers expressly tuned to the subjects, and felicity of language both in the sound and the significance of words employed. Yet in the first line of the verse above quoted the far-sought elegance of characteristic description in the 'breezy call of incense-breathing morn' is spoiled utterly by the disagreeable clash between

THE ELEGY.

'breezy' and 'breathing' within a few syllables of each other. Contrast this with the corresponding line, and the dullest ear will distinguish the clear full harmony of 'the cock's shrill clarion and the echoing horn'."—James Montgomery's *Lectures*, p. 204.

Gray first wrote this sta. as follows:

"For ever sleep; the breezy call of morn,
 Or swallow twittering from the straw-built shed,
 Or chanticleer so shrill, or echoing horn,
 No more shall rouse them from their lowly bed."

Incense-breathing morn. Cf. Byron:

"The morn is up again, the dewy morn,
 With breath all incense, and with cheek all bloom."

Milton, *P. L.*, IX. 292:

"Now when as sacred light began to dawn
 In Eden on the humid flowers that breathed
 Their morning incense."

Milton, *Arcades*, 56: "the odorous breath of morn."
Milton, *P. L.*, IV. 641:

"Sweet is the breath of morn, her rising sweet
 With charm of earliest birds."

Incense-breathing. Explain this epithet.

18 Straw-built shed. In this expression there is a reference to the thatched roofs common in England.

Shed. For meaning cf. *Traveller*, l. 162.

19 The cock's shrill clarion. Cf. Milton, *P. L.*, VII. 443:

"The crested cock, whose clarion sounds
 The silent hours."

Hamlet, I. 1: "The cock that is the trumpet to the morn."

Clarion. Lat. *clarus*, clear; Fr. *clairon*, a kind of trumpet. Here it means the crowing of the cock, by metonymy.

Cf. Milton:

"The warlike sound
 Of trumpets loud and clarions."

Echoing was written by Gray, *ecchoing*.

Echoing horn. The chase usually began early in the morning.

20 Shall. Why *shall* and not *will*?

Lowly bed. Chambers says: "Really the *bed*, not metaphorically used for the *grave*, as has been supposed." Wakefield remarks: "Some readers, keeping in mind the *narrow cell* above, have mistaken the *lowly bed* in this verse for the grave—a most puerile and ridiculous blunder;" and Mitford says: "Here the epithet *lowly* as applied to *bed*, occasions some ambiguity as to whether the poet meant the bed on which they sleep, or the grave in which they are laid, which in poetry is called a *lowly bed*. Of course the former is designed."

This sta. furnishes an example of the figure, accumulation, and also of euphemism.

21-24 Cf. Thomson, *Winter*, 311:

"In vain for him the officious wife prepares
The fire fair blazing, and the vestment warm;
In vain his little children, peeping out
Into the mingling storm, demand their sire
With tears of artless innocence."

21 Shall. What change in the meaning would arise from substituting *will* for *shall*?

22 Housewife. Gray wrote *huswife*.

Ply her care=*ply her task* or *object of care*. Mitford says: "To *ply a care* is an expression that is not proper to our language, and was probably formed for the rhyme, *share*."

Cf. Scott, *Lady of the Lake*, VI. 17:

"For life! for life! their plight they ply."

23 No children run. Cf. Burn's *Cotter's Sat. Night*:

"Th' expectant wee things, toddlin', stacher through
  To meet their dad, wi' flichterin' noise and glee.
His wee-bit ingle blinkin' bonnilie,
  His clean hearth-stane, his thrifty wifie's smile,
The lisping infant prattlin' on his knee,
  Does a' his weary carking cares beguile."

Cf. *Traveller*, l. 191-198.

Sire. For derivation see note on *Traveller*, l. 229.

24 Envied kiss, a MS. variation gives it "coming kiss."
Cf. Virgil, *Georgics*, II. 523:

"Interea dulces pendent circum oscula nati."

Dryden:

"Whose little arms about thy legs are cast,
  And climbing for a kiss prevent their mother's haste."

THE ELEGY.

Thomson, *Liberty*, III. 171 :
"His little children climbing for a kiss."
To share, etc., forms an adverbiul extension of *climbs*.
25 Sickle. A. S. *sicel, sicol;* Ger. *sichel;* Gr. ζάγκλη; Lat. *secula*.
26 Furrow. A. S. *fur* or *furh;* Ger. *furche*.
Stubborn. One authority makes this word come from *stout-born;* a second, from Gr. στιβαρός, thick, stout, sturdy; and a third, from *stub*, a thick, short stock. The last appears the most probable.
Cf. Dryden : "Take a plant of stubborn oak."
Glebe=the earth, soil. Lat., It., Sp., *gleba*, a clod.
Cf. Gay, *Fables*, II. 15 :
"'Tis mine to tame the stubborn glebe."
Has broke. See note on *Traveller*, l. 358.
This is ungrammatical, being a violation of "sequence of tense." See the other lines of the sta. Why did he write thus?
Furrow=plough, by metonymy. Point out other figures in this sta.
27 Jocund. Lat. *jocundus*, from *jocus*, a jest. By poetic licence for *jocundly*=merrily.
Afield. In this and other similar adverbs, the *a* represents some preposition, as "in," "an," "of," contracted by rapidity of pronunciation.
See *Shaks. Gram.*, par. 24.
Cf. Gay : "Afield I went amid the morning dew."
Dryden, *Virgil's Ecl.*, II. 38 : "With me to drive afield."
Milton, *Lycidas*, 27 : "We drove afield."
Sturdy. O. Fr. *estourdi;* Fr. *étourdi*, stunned, astonished.
Cf. Spenser, *Shep. Kal. Feb.*:
"But to the roote bent his sturdy stroake,
And made many wounds in the wast (wasted) oake."
Dryden, *Georgics*, III. 639 :
"Labor him with many a sturdy stroke."
29 Ambition. *Ambition* and *grandeur* are used for the "ambitious and the grand," and (like "memory" in the tenth sta.) are instances of the figure, metonymy

For grammatical relation of *ambition* and *grandeur*, see note on *Traveller*, l. 41.

Mock. Gr. μωκάομαι; Fr. *moquer*.

Cf. *Othello*, III. 3 :
"O, beware, my lord, of jealousy ;
It is the green-eyed monster which doth mock
The meat it feeds on."

30 Their homely joys. A MS. reading gives *rustic joys*.

Homely=plain, having the plainness of home. Cf. Shaks., "A homely house"; Dryden, "Homely fare"; Burns, "What tho' on hamely fare we dine."

Destiny obscure, an example of hyperbaton.

31 Disdainful smile. Cf. Roget, "Derisive smile."

32 Simple. Lat. *simplex; sine*, without, and *plica*, a fold; or, *semel*, once, and *plicare*, to fold; It. *semplice;* Sp. and Fr. *simple*.

"In simple manners all the secret lies."

Annals, originally records classified by years. Lat. *annales*, chronicles, from *annus*, a year.

Poor. Would modern usage allow this word to be considered singular?

In this sta. will be noticed the imperfect rhymes, *toil* and *smile; obscure* and *poor*.

What are the requirements of perfect rhyme?

Quote other examples of imperfect rhymes in the *Elegy*.

33 The boast . . grave. Mr. Mathias, the author of *The Pursuits of Literature*, terms this *the* great sta. of the *Elegy*, and the Earl of Carlisle says : "All sermons are here concentrated; and here every expression comes up to the dignity of the most solemn of all human themes, without the slightest strain or inflation."

Mitford suggests that Gray had in mind these verses from his friend West's *Monody on Queen Caroline:*

"Ah, me! what boots us all our boasted power,
  Our golden treasure and our purple state ;
They cannot wait the inevitable hour,
  Nor stay the fearful violence of fate."

Cf. Horace, *Odes*, Bk. I. 4-13 :

"Pallida mors æquo pulsat pede pauperum tabernas
  Regumque turres."

THE ELEGY.

The boast of heraldry. The assumed superiority of those who, from their high rank, are entitled to coats of arms.

Heraldry. Ger. *herold;* It. *araldo;* Sp. *heraldo;* Fr. *herault.*

Heraldry, or the science of armorial bearings, is supposed to have had its origin among the French knights towards the close of the twelfth century. The shields before this time presented a plain face of polished metal, but "that no Norman might perish by the hand of another nor one Frenchman kill another" certain devices, rude at first, were outlined on the shield. It is difficult to say when these devices assumed that hereditary character essential to the idea of armorial bearings. The transmission of arms from father to son was recognized during the thirteenth century.

At first, every knight assumed what arms he pleased. Animals, plants, imaginary monsters, etc., were fixed upon, as taste or fancy dictated; and, whenever it was possible, the object chosen was one whose name bore sufficient resemblance in sound to suggest the name or title of the bearer of it. As might be expected, the result was the utmost confusion, which was however reduced to a system during the thirteenth and fourteenth centuries. After this time none were allowed to assume coats of arms without consulting their sovereign, or king-at-arms; nor then were they permitted to do so unless they could claim a certain rank, or unless the devices chosen were held to be suitable, not infringing in any way on those of others.

Pomp. Gr. $\pi o \mu \pi \eta$, from $\pi \acute{\epsilon} \mu \pi \omega$, to send; Lat., It., and Sp., *pompa;* Fr. *pompe.*

Cf. Addison: "The pomps of a Roman triumph."

Milton: "The bright pomp ascended jubilant."

Shaks., *Othello*, III. 3:
"Farewell . . . .
Pride, pomp, and circumstance of glorious war."

Power. Lat. *posse*, to be able; *potis*, able, and *esse*, to be; Fr. *pouvoir.*

35 Await. Gray's MS. and an edition of 1768 have *awaits*, but this cannot be justified on grammatical grounds.

Alike. The great, the noble, the fair and the rich can no more escape death than the poor. *Alike* is an adverb.

36 The paths . . grave. A Canadian will insensibly associate this line with the memory of Wolfe. See *Fifth Reader*, Campbells' series, page 243, and observe Wolfe's testi-

THE ELEGY. 111

mony to the genuine poetry of the *Elegy:* "I would rather have written those lines than take Quebec to-morrow:" Wolfe's own fate is a striking illustration of the truth contained in this line.

But=only, adverbial to the phrase, *to the grave.*

37 Nor you . . raise. These two lines were first written:

"Forgive, ye proud, th' involuntary fault,
If memory to these no trophies raise."

Nor . . fault. Mitford says: "This has always appeared to me to be a very flat and unpoetical expression."

These. Who?

Ye has here a demonstrative force.

38 Memory=remembering ones.

Trophies. Gr. $\tau\rho\delta\pi\alpha\iota o\nu$; $\tau\rho o\pi\eta$, a turn; $\tau\rho\acute{\epsilon}\pi\omega$, to turn; Lat. *tropæum*; Fr. *trophée.*

Cf. Shaks.:

"There lie thy bones
Till we with trophies do adorn thy tomb."

Originally, trophies were memorials of victory erected on the spot where the enemy had turned to flight. These memorials consisted of helmets, shields, etc., placed upon the trunk of a tree, or upon a mound raised for that purpose. Gradually these memorials came to be preserved in some temple. And finally, on the death of any individual, distinguished especially for warlike achievements, the memorials were suspended over, or placed above his tomb.

39 Where . . praise. This clause is adverbial to *raise.*

Long-drawn aisle. "This expression pictures the long narrow vista of the aisle of a cathedral or large church."—Chambers.

Aisle. Lat. *ala,* a wing; Fr. *aile.* Gray wrote it *ile.*

Fretted. Fret is a kind of angular ornament, formed by small fillets interlacing each other at right angles. Parker in his *Glossary of Architecture* derives the word from the Lat. *fretum,* a strait; another derivation suggested is Lat. *ferrum,* iron. It. *ferrata,* an iron grating. The most natural derivation seems to be A. S. *frætwian,* to adorn; *frætu,* an ornament.

Cf. Milton: "The roof was fretted gold."

Vault=arched roof or ceiling; Lat. *volvere, volutus,* to roll; Fr. *voûte.*

THE ELEGY.

40 Pealing anthem. Cf. *Il Pens.*, 161:
"There let the pealing organ blow
To the full-voiced quire below,
In service high, and anthem clear."
Pealing=resounding. Lat. *pello*, to beat or strike, as drums;
A. S. *bellan*, to bellow.

Anthem. Gr. *ἀντί*, in return, and *ὕμνος*, a song;
hence literally, that which is sung in alternate parts.

"A species of musical composition introduced into the service of the English Church after the Reformation and appointed to be sung daily, at morning and evening service, after the third collect. The words of the Anthem are taken from the Psalms, or other suitable parts of the Scriptures, and the music is either for solo, soli, or chorus, or a mixture of all three. As a specimen of English music, it can only be heard to perfection in cathedral service."—Chambers's *Encyclopædia*.

These two lines 39, 40, are a periphrasis for 'in the church.'

41 Storied. Gr. *ἱστορία*, a history; *ἵστωρ*, knowing;
Lat. *historia*; A. S. *stær*, *ster*.

Cf. *Il Pens.*, 159: "Storied windows richly dight."
Scott, *Lady of the Lake:* "Storied pane."

Animated=lifelike. Cf. Pope, *Temple of Fame*, 73:
"Heroes in animated marble frown."
Virgil, *Æneid*, VI. 847: "spirantia æra."

42 Mansion. Lat. *mansio*, a dwelling, from *maneo*, to abide; Fr. *maison*. Cf. *Traveller*, ll. 167, 201.

43 Honor's voice. What does this mean?

Provoke. Mitford thinks this use of the word "unusually bold, to say the least." But observe the derivation. Cf. Pope:

"But when our country's cause provokes to arms."

Rolfe remarks: "It is simply the etymological meaning, *to call forth*; Lat. *provocare*." This is certainly a mistake, for it evidently means to awaken the silent dust to animation.

The dull cold ear. Cf. Shaks., *Henry VIII.*, III. 2:
"And sleep in dull cold marble."

Notice the instances of the figure, interrogation, in this sta. What other figures in it?

THE ELEGY.

45 Perhaps .. lyre. Carlisle remarks: "this is said with most elegant truth."

Neglected. In what sense is this epithet used?

46 Pregnant .. fire. Cf. Cowper's *Boadicea*:

"Such the bard's prophetic words,
Pregnant with celestial fire,
Bending as he swept the chords
Of his sweet but awful lyre."

Rolfe charges Cowper with having copied the second line of the above sta.

Pregnant. Lat. *prægnans*, contracted from *præ-genans*, from *præ* and *gignere*, to beget. Cf. *Traveller*, l. 138.

47 Hands .. sway'd. Mitford quotes Ovid, *Ep.* V. 86:

"Sunt mihi, quas possint sceptra decere, manus."

Hands. With *hands* supply *are laid*, etc.

Rod of empire. Gray also wrote "reins of empire."

Sway'd. A. S. *wæge*, a pair of scales; *wæg*, a wave; Ger. *schwingen*, to swing.

Cf. Shaks.: "The will of man is by his reason swayed."

48 Wak'd. Supply *that might have*.

Living lyre. Cf. Cowley:

"Begin the song and strike the living lyre."

Pope, *Windsor Forest*, 281:

"Who now shall charm the shades where Cowley strung
His living harp, and lofty Denham sung?"

Paraphrase this sta. so as to distinguish clearly the force of ll. 46 and 48.

50 Rich .. time. This phrase is adjectival to *page*.

Spoils. Give meaning in this connection.

Unroll—Lat. *revolvere*. This word carries the mind back to the *volumes* of the ancients, each "book" having to be opened in the same way as we open a map by *unroll*ing it.

51 Penury. Gr. $\pi\varepsilon\hat{\imath}\nu\alpha$, hunger; Lat., It., Sp., *penuria;* Fr. *pénurie*.

Repress'd. Another MS. reading was *depress'd*.

Rage=enthusiasm, inspiration; that is, the enthusiasm by which they might have been carried to eminence in one or other of the lofty positions indicated in the previous sta. Lat. *rabies;* Fr. *rage.*

Cf. Collins, *The Passions,* 110:

"Thy humblest reed could more prevail,
Had more of strength, diviner rage,
Than all which charms this laggard age."

52 Genial current. Their necessitous circumstances prevented the full development and exercise of the talents with which they were gifted by nature.

Genial has here its etymological meaning, from *gigno,* of *inborn* or *natural.*

53 Full . . bear. Cf. Bishop Hall, *Contemplations:* "There is many a rich storre laid up in the bowells of the earth, many a fair pearle in the bosome of the sea, that never was seene, nor never shall bee." So Milton in his *Comus* speaks of the

"Sea-girt isles,
That like to rich and various gems, inlay
The unadorned bosom of the deep."

Shakes., *Richard III.,* I. 4:

"Inestimable stones, unvalued jewels,
All scattered in the bottom of the sea.
Some lay in dead men's skulls; and in those holes
Where eyes did once inhabit, there were crept
As 'twere in scorn of eyes, reflecting gems,
That wooed the slimy bottom of the deep."

Full, an adverb qualifying *many.*

Many. See note on l. 198 of the *Traveller.*

Gem. Lat., It., *gemma;* Sp. *yema,* a bud; Fr. *gemme;* A. S. *gim,* a jewel.

Purest ray serene. Carlisle is afraid "that *purest ray serene* is what would be called at school a *botch.*" But Cf. Milton, *Hymn on Nat.:* "flower-inwoven tresses torn." *Comus:* "beckoning shadows dire," "every alley green." *L'Allegro:* "Native wood-notes wild." *Lycidas:* "Blest kingdoms meek." From these expressions it will be seen that if it is a *botch,* Gray is sinning in good company.

Serene=clear or bright.

55 Full . . air. Cf. Pope, *Rape of the Lock,* IV. 158:

"Like roses that in deserts bloom and die."

Mitford quotes Chamberlayne, *Pharonida*, II. 4:
"Like beauteous flowers which vainly waste their scent
Of odours in unhaunted deserts."

Cf. Young, *Love of Fame*, Sat. V. 228:
"In distant wilds, by human eyes unseen,
She rears her flowers, and spreads her velvet green;
Pure gurgling rills the lonely desert trace,
And waste their music on the savage race."

Philip, *Thule:*
"Like woodland flowers, which paint the desert glades,
And waste their sweets in unfrequented shades."

Churchill, *Gotham*, II. 20:
"Nor waste their sweetness in the desert air."

To blush=to blossom. A. S. *ablisian.*
Cowper:
"Modest and ingenuous worth
That blushed at its own praise."

To blush is adverbial to *is born*.

Unseen is the complement of *to blush*.

56 Waste. Gray spelt this word, *wast*. Parse *waste*.

On the desert air. Cf. *Macbeth*, IV. 3:
"That would be howl'd out in the desert air."

The unfathom'd caves of ocean . . desert air. These terms are aptly chosen to represent the deep poverty and the unappreciative surroundings which often obscure the 'lamp of genius.'

57 Some . . breast. "What son of Freedom is not in raptures with this tribute of praise to such an exalted character, in immortal verse? This honorable testimony and the noble detestation of arbitrary power, with which it is accompanied, might possibly be one cause of Dr. Johnson's animosity against our poet. Upon this topic the critic's feelings, we know, were irritability itself and 'tremblingly alive all o'er.'¦"—Wakefield.

Gray first wrote this line "Cato, who," but by a happy afterthought substituted "Hampden, that." So also instead "Milton" he at first wrote "Tully," and instead of "Cromwell," "Cæsar." It is said that Mason suggested these judicious changes.

THE ELEGY.

Some village Hampden. An instance of the figure, antonomasia. Cf. *Milton* and *Cromwell*, ll. 59, 60.

Hampden. John Hampden, cousin of Oliver Cromwell, entered Parliament in 1621, was imprisoned in 1627 for refusing to pay his proportion of an illegal loan which the king was attempting to raise, was shortly afterwards liberated and became an active member of Parliament. In 1634, to raise money, Charles had recourse to the impost of "ship-money"; at first limiting the tax to London and the maritime towns; but attempting in 1636 to levy from inland places, Hampden resisted, was tried, and fined. He was afterwards a member of both the Short and Long Parliaments, and was one of the " Five" Charles tried to seize. On the breaking out of the civil war, he entered the Parliamentary army, and was fatally wounded at the battle of Chalgrove Field.

Dauntless. Lat., *domito*, to subdue; Fr. *dompter;* probably from Gr. $\delta\alpha\mu\acute{\alpha}\omega$.

58 Little tyrant. The wealthy landed proprietor who sought to oppress his tenantry, as Charles I. attempted to violate the liberties of the English people.

Milton. The great English Epic poet (1608-1674). Enumerate M.'s writings.

60 Cromwell. From the Revolution till the present time, there have been many who, like our poet, have not hesitated to charge Cromwell with the murder of Charles I./ That the act was illegal and unjustifiable no one will doubt, but as to the culpability of Cromwell there will always be a difference of opinion. On the one hand, it is urged that Cromwell had England then, as thoroughly as he ever had, within the grasp of his iron will, and that he should therefore have controlled the country in this matter; on the other hand, it is asseverated that the current was too strong for even Cromwell, and that for his own safety and for the peace of the country he was compelled to be accessory to the "crime."

In the preceding sta., the poet implies that circumstances are needed to produce eminent men. Discuss this sentiment.

61 The applause .. flame. The "infinitives," *to command, to despise, to scatter, to read,* with their complements, are the immediate "objects" of *forbade* in line 69. By supplying the remote object, *them,* the construction will be evident. These infinitives, with their complements, are intended by the poet to represent 'their growing virtues.' Their (lot) not only circumscribed their virtues, but also confined their crimes, namely,

THE ELEGY. 117

to wade, etc., to shut, etc., to hide, etc., to quench, etc., to heap, etc. These infinitives are the objects of *forbade* in l. 67.

The applause . . command. The aspirings of the 'rude forefathers' for political leadership were effectually crushed by their poverty and lack of knowledge.

62 The threats . . despise. The poor, having all that they thought worth living for, in their limited 'fields' and in their family joys, could not afford to defy the party in power; but for the sake of their 'little all' yielded quietly to those holding or professing to hold authority.

Threats. Cf. Milton: "Those rigid threats of death."

Pain. A. S. *pin*, pain; *pinan*, to punish; Ger. *pein;* Gr. ποινή, penalty; Lat. *pœna*, penalty; Fr. *peine*.

63 To scatter . . land. The particular reference probably is to the government of Walpole, who, holding power during a lengthy and prosperous period of English history, had been forced to yield up the 'rod of empire' in 1742, amidst the regrets and encomiums of his admirers.

Cf. Tickell: "To scatter blessings o'er the British land."

Smiling may mean *productive* as applied to the land itself, or by the figure, metonymy, may signify *prosperous* or *grateful*, in reference to the people.

64 To read . . eyes. Their lot prevented them from identifying themselves so thoroughly with the great general interests of the nation as to lead it to evidence its admiration by manifestations of gratification.

65 Lot forbade. The natural order of these words would place them at the beginning of the preceding sta.—an example of anastrophe.

Alone is connected grammatically with *virtues*.

66 Growing virtues. The powers of mind that would have developed themselves if an opportunity had been afforded.

Crimes. Gr. κρίμα, a matter for judgment; κρίνω, to separate, to judge; Lat. *crimen;* *cerno*, to judge; Fr. *crime*.

67 Forbade . . mankind. "These two verses are specimens of sublimity of the purest kind, like the simple grandeur of Hebrew poetry; depending solely on the thought, unassisted by epithets and the artificial decorations of expression."—*Cleveland*.

Wade. A. S. *wadan;* Ger. *waten;* Gr. βαίνω; Lat. *vado;* Fr. *guéer*.

THE ELEGY.

To wade .. them. Cf. Pope, *Temple of Fame*, 347.
" And swam to empire through the purple flood."

68 To shut .. mankind. That is, to act cruelly and oppressively. Cf. Shakes., *Hen. V.*, III. 3 :
"The gates of mercy shall be all shut up."

Mercy. Fr. *merci;* contracted from Lat. *misericordia*.

69 The struggling .. hide. In their low 'estate' there was no temptation for them to conceal their real sentiments, as is too frequently the case with those who are acquiring or have acquired position and influence. In covering up one's real opinions, "conscious truth," for the sake of place or power, there must be more or less of a 'struggle' and "pang" in the mind.

70 To quench .. shame. Cf. Shakes., *W. T.*, IV. 3.
"Come quench your blushes, and present yourself."

These 'rude' ones were unpractised in hiding the guilt of the heart under a fair exterior.

71 To heap .. flame. The poets, 'rude' and poor though they were, would not degrade their 'unlettered muse' by singing at the command of the wealthy or haughty. It is evidently implied that too many poets by their sycophantic adulations of 'Luxury' and 'Pride' won and maintained a prominence without possessing real worth. It will be remembered that Gray refused the "Laurel."

Heap. A MS. variation gives *crown*.

72 Shrine. A. S. *scrin;* Ger. *schrein;* Lat. *scrinium*, a basket or chest ; Fr. *écrin*.

Paraphrase ll. 71, 72.

Incense=Poetic adulation or flattery.

Muse. The muses were, according to the earliest writers, the inspiring goddesses of song, and, according to later notions, divinities presiding over the different kinds of poetry, and over the arts and sciences. Their names and provinces were :— Clio, the muse of history ; Euterpe, the muse of lyric poetry ; Thalia, the muse of comedy ; Melpomene, the muse of tragedy ; Terpsichore, the muse of choral dance, &c. ; Polymnia, the muse of sublime hymn ; Urania, the muse of astronomy ; and Calliope, the muse of epic poetry.

After this, the 18th, stanza, Gray's first MS. had the following four stas., now omitted :

THE ELEGY.

"The thoughtless world to majesty may bow,
  Exalt the brave, and idolize success ;
But more to innocence their safety owe
  Than Pow'r, or Genius, e'er conspir'd to bless.

"And thou who, mindful of the unhonor'd dead,
  Dost in these notes their artless tale relate,
By night and lonely contemplation led
  To wander in the gloomy walks of fate.

"Hark ! how the sacred calm, that breathes around,
  Bids every fierce tumultuous passion cease ;
In still small accents whisp'ring from the ground
  A grateful earnest of eternal peace.

"No more, with reason and thyself at strife,
  Give anxious cares and wishes room ;
But through the cool sequester'd vale of life
  Pursue the silent tenor of thy doom."

Gray first intended that the *Elegy* should end here. The second of these stas. has been remodelled and used as the 24th of the present version.

73 Far .. strife. Cf. Drummond :

"Far from the madding worldling's hoarse discords."

To give the poet's meaning, this line must be taken as an adverbial adjunct of *kept*. If it be taken with the second line, as by punctuation and position it should be, it would ."give a sense exactly contrary to that intended." They attended to their own little matters, unaffected by the eager scrambling for wealth or position that must necessarily exist in every town or city.

Far. An adverb qualifying the phrase *from strife*.

Madding=Excited and exciting.

Ignoble strife. Gray despised a commercial life.

74 Their .. stray. Is a principal clause.

To stray. The object of *learn'd*.

75 Cool vale of life. Cf. Pope, *Epitaph on Fenton :*

"Foe to loud praise, and friend to learned ease
  Content with science in the vale of peace."

Cool. Why ?

Sequester'd=Retired.

77 Yet, an adverb qualifying *implores*.
E'en emphasizes *these bones*. Cf. *Traveller*, l. 260.
These bones=the bones of these.
To protect. This infinitive has an adverbial relation to erected.
78 Still erected=formerly set up and still standing.
79 With . . decked, an adjunct of *memorial*.
Uncouth. A. S. *un*, and *cuth*, the past participle of *cunnan* to know. The literal meaning is, 'unknown.' Render it here, 'unpolished.' Cf. *L'Allegro*, 5: "uncouth cell"; *P. L.*, V. 98. "Voyage uncouth" (unknown); *Lyc.* 186, "uncouth swain."
Rhymes. A.S. *rim, gerim*, a number; Ger. *reim*, It. and Sp. *rima*. The *h* appears to have crept in from analogy to *rhythm*.
Shapeless sculpture. "In Gray's *Elegy* is there an image more striking than his 'shapeless sculpture?'"—Byron.
Shapeless, not as being without shape, but as having little resemblance to the object intended to be represented.
Deck'd=adorned or decorated. A. S. *decan*, or *theccan;* Ger. *decken;* Gr. στέγω; Lat. *tego;* Cf. Lat. *decus.* For the sound of the *d* see note on *Traveller*, l. 155.
80 Passing tribute of a sigh. This may mean simply the trifling tribute of a sigh, or better, the sigh forced from the passer-by.
81 Spelt. Account for the spelling of this word? Would you give the same reason as for *deckt?*
82 Fame. Gr. φήμη, fame, from φημι, to say; Lat., It. and Sp. *fama;* Fr. *fame.*
Elegy. The first reading was *epitaph*.
Fame and elegy. What is meant?
Text. This refers to a common practice of inscribing passages of Scripture on the tomb-stones.

84 That teach. "As this construction is not, as it now stands, correct, I think Gray originally wrote "*to teach*," but altered it afterwards, *euphoniæ gratia*, and made the grammar give way to the sound."—Mitford.
Others would justify it as a "construction according to sense." This seems unnecessary, since it is not in accordance with the best usage.

THE ELEGY.

To die is the immediate, **moralist**, the remote or dative object of *teach*.

Rustic moralist. This may mean either the peasant who practises morality, or the one who simply philosophizes thereupon. How do you reconcile the fact of the rustic reading the inscriptions with what is implied in l. 115?

85 For who, etc. Carlisle says "there is much tender beauty" in this and the succeeding sta.

"No, sir, there are but two good stanzas in Gray's poetry, which are in his 'Elegy in a Country Church-yard.' He then repeated the stanza:

'For who to dumb forgetfulness a prey,' etc.

mistaking one word; for instead of *precincts* he said *confines*. He added, 'The other stanza I forget.'"—Boswell's *Johnson*.

For is merely an introductory particle, being unnecessary to complete the sense.

Prey is in apposition with *being*. The meaning of this and the following line is "whoever willingly resigned this life of pleasure and anxiety to be utterly neglected and forgotten"?

Who .. e'er, for *whoever*, an instance of tmesis.

87 Warm. Why?

Precincts=limits or confines. Lat. *præ*, before, *cingere*, to gird.

Cheerful. Gr. χαρά, joy; Fr. *chère*, entertainment; Gray wrote *chearful*. See Earle's *Philology*, sec. 181-7.

88 Nor cast .. behind. Supply *that*. This clause is adjectival to *whoever* the subject of the preceding.

Notice the happy effect of alliteration. Cf. Byron,

"Foremost, fighting fell."

There are several other instances of this poetic artifice in the the *Elegy*. Quote them.

89 On .. fires. This sta. contains an example of climax. We have death, after death, after burial, and even after that.

Parting. See note on l. 1.

90 Pious=affectionate. Lat. *pius;* Cf. Ovid, "piæ lacrimæ; Horace, "debita lacrima." Pope, *Elegy on an Unfortunate Lady*, 49:

"No friend's complaint, no kind domestic tear
Pleas'd thy pale ghost, or grac'd thy mournful bier;
By foreign hands thy dying eyes were closed."

THE ELEGY.

91 E'en, an adverb emphasizing the phrase, *from the tomb*.
92 There were several readings for this line before the final selection was made:

"And buried ashes glow with social fires."
"And in our ashes glow," etc.

Mason says: "In the first edition it stood.

'Awake and faithful to her wonted fires,'

"and I think rather better. He means to say in plain prose, that we wish to be remembered by our friends after our death, in the same manner as when alive we wished to be remembered by them in our absence; this would be expressed clearer, if the metaphorical term 'fires' was rejected, and the line run thus:

'Awake and faithful to her first desires.'

I do not put this alteration down for the idle vanity of aiming to amend the passage, but purely to explain it."

Mitford paraphrases this couplet thus: "The voice of Nature still cries from the tomb in the language of the epitaph inscribed upon it, which still endeavors to connect us with the living; the fires of former affection are still alive beneath our ashes." Cf. Chaucer, *C. T.*, 3880:

"Yet in our ashes cold is fire yreken" (raked).

Gray himself quotes Petrarch, *Sonnet* 169.

Ashes. Explain how the term *ashes* comes to mean *bodily remains*.

93 For thee .. fate. This sta. originally stood thus:

"If chance that e'er some pensive spirit more,
  By sympathetic musings here delay'd,
  With vain, though kind inquiry shall explore
  Thy once-lov'd haunt, this long-deserted shade."

For thee, connected with *may say* in l. 97. In this construction, *Haply .. say* is the principal clause; *If .. fate*, is subordinate adverbial to it.

Thee. Does this mean Gray himself?
Unhonor'd dead. Cf. *neglected spot*, l. 45.
94 Artless. Give the force of this word.
95 Chance=perchance, an adverb.
Lonely, contracted from *alonely*=all-one (ly).
By .. led, an attributive adjunct of *spirit*.

THE ELEGY.

Contemplation. Milton,
"For contemplation he, and valor formed."

96 Kindred, from *kin*, A.S. *cyn*, kin; Ger. *kind*, a child; Gr. γεννάω, to beget; γένος race; Lat. *nascor*, to be born; *genus*, race; Fr. *genre*.

Some kindred spirit, that is some one of a similar, meditative nature.

98 Peep of dawn. Cf. Milton, *Comus*, 138:

"Ere the blabbing eastern scout
The nice morn, on the Indian steep
From her cabin'd loop-hole peep."

99 Brushing .. lawn. This phrase is adjectival to *him*. Cf. Milton, *Arcades*, 50:

"And from the boughs brush off the evil dew."

P. L., V. 428:

"Though from off the boughs each morn,
We brush mellifluous flowers."

100 Upland lawn=an area of grass at the summit of a hill. This line was first written thus:

"On the high brow of yonder hanging lawn."

Lawn, which is only another form of land, is now generally understood to mean a level grassy surface in front of or around a house.

Cf. *Traveller*, l. 319.

101 The following excellent sta. came in here in Gray's first MS., but was afterwards omitted:

"Him have we seen the greenwood side along,
  While o'er the heath we hied, our labour done,
Oft as the woodlark pip'd her farewell song,
  With wistful eyes pursue the setting sun."

Mason said: "I rather wonder that he rejected this stanza, as it not only has the same sort of Doric delicacy which charms us peculiarly in this part of the poem, but also completes the account of his whole day; whereas, this evening scene being omitted, we have only his morning walk, and his noontide repose."

Nodding. In botany this term means drooping, and was probably suggested by Gray's botanical studies.

1C2 Fantastic roots. The roots of an old beech often rise above the ground, and assume curiously twisted forms.
Cf. Spenser, *Ruines of Rome*, sta. 28:
"Showing her wreathed roots and naked armes."
103 His listless length, etc. Spenser's *Brittain's Ida*, III. 2:
"Her goodly length stretcht on a lilly-bed."
Noontide—the time of noon.
Noon. A. S. *non;* Old Ger. *none;* Old Fr. *none.* Supposed to be derived from Lat. *nona (hora)*, the ninth hour, at which the chief meal of the Romans was eaten.
Tide=time. A. S. *tid,* time; *tidan,* to happen; Ger. *zeit,* time.
104 Babbles. Heb. *bavel,* confusion; Gr. $\beta\alpha\beta\alpha'\varphi\omega$, to prattle; Fr. *babiller;* Ger. *babbeln.* Cf. Horace, *Od.* III. 13:
"unde loquaces
Lymphæ desiliunt tuæ."
Thomson, *Spring,* 644:
"Divided by a babbling brook."
105 Hard .. scorn. Another reading is:
"With gestures quaint, now smiling as in scorn."
Hard by—near by, close by.
Hard is an adverb modifying the phrase following.
Smiling as in scorn, a participial phrase adjectival to the subject *he.*
As in scorn, analyze thus:—*as (he would smile) (if he were smiling) in scorn.*
Cf. Skelton, *Prol. to B. of C.*:
"Smylynge half in scorne
At our foly."
106 Muttering .. fancies, adverbial to *would rove.*
See *How to Parse,* par. 261.
The first MS. had *would he rove.*
107 Drooping .. love. Attributive adjunct of *he* (understood), the subject of *would rove* to be supplied.
Smiling, drooping. These words express the varied moods in which the youth is alternately found:—*now smiling, now drooping.*

THE ELEGY.

Woeful-wan. In Gray's corrected MS. this is written *woeful-wan*. If this be accepted as the correct reading, then the compound epithet will mean *woefully wan*, that is, *wan* to such a degree as to indicate a feeling of woe or intense misery. If written without the hyphen the expression must be taken to mean *woeful* and *wan*.

Woeful-wan is adjectival to *he*.

Like, here an adjective qualifying *he*.

One. Parsed as an indefinite pronoun in the objective case after *to* understood.

108 Craz'd, cross'd, like *forlorn* qualify *one*.

109 On. Gray first wrote *from*.

Custom'd = accustom'd. This word is now obsolete in this sense.

110 Near. Parse. See note on l. 11.

111 Another came. Another morn came.

Rill, contracted from Lat. *rivulus*.

Cf. Milton:
"From a thousand petty rills."

Wood. In what sense used?

113 The next (morn came).

With . . array, an adverbial phrase connected with *borne*.

Dirges. From *dirige*, a solemn service in the Catholic Church, being a hymn beginning *dirige gressus meos*.

Due. Lat. *debere*, to owe; Fr. *dû*, past participle of *devoir*, to owe.

Array. Cf. meaning in *Traveller*, l. 171.

114 Slow=slowly, an adverb qualifying *borne*.

Church-way path.

Cf. Shaks., *Mids. N. Dream*, V. 2:
"Now it is the time of night,
That the graves all gaping wide,
Every one lets forth his sprite
In the churchway paths to glide."

Church-way path=church-yard path.

Church.—Gr. κύριος, a lord; οἶκος, a house. Cf. A. S. *circe*.

Him borne. See note on *Traveller*, l. 41.

115 For merely introduces the parenthetical clause.

THE ELEGY.

For thou canst. This parenthetical clause implies that the 'hoary-headed swain' himself could not read.

Lay. A. S. *ley*, a song; Ger. *lied*; It. *lai*; Old Fr. *lai*, *lais*, from Lat. *lessus*, a funeral lamentation.

The exigencies of rhyme compelled Gray to use this word in place of *epitaph*.

116 Grav'd. Why not *graven?* A. S. *grafan*; Ger. *graben*; Gr. γράφω; Fr. *graver*.

Before the epitaph, the MS. contains the following omitted sta.:

"There scattered oft, the earliest of the year,
By hands unseen are frequent violets found;
The robin loves to build and warble there,
And little footsteps lightly print the ground."

"This stanza was printed in some of the first editions, but afterwards omitted because Mr. Gray thought (and in my opinion very justly) that it was too long a parenthesis in this place. The lines, however, are in themselves exquisitely fine, and demand preservation."—Mason. Gray himself in writing to Dr. Beattie in regard to this omission, said: "As to description, I have always thought that it made the most graceful ornament of poetry, but never ought to make the subject."

117 Lap of Earth. Cf. Spenser, *F. Q.*, V. 7:

"For other beds the priests there used none,
But on their Mother Earth's deare lap did lie."

Milton, *P. L.*, X. 777:

"How glad would lay me down,
As in my mother's lap."

By this beautiful figure (metaphor) he is made to rest in his grave (the lap of earth) like a tired child in the lap of its mother.

118 Youth, the subject of *rests*.

119 Frown'd not=smiled, an example of litotes.

120 Melancholy. See note on *Traveller*, l. 1.

For=as, and is redundant. See *How to Parse*, par. 209.

Her own. See note on *Traveller*, l. 30.

121 Large was his bounty. An instance of hyperbaton.

Sincere, usually derived from Lat. *sine*, without, and *cera*, wax, meaning honey free from wax.

122 As is here used absolutely, not correlatively.

THE ELEGY.

Largely=large. Why so written?

123 Which is the appositive, *all* or *tear* ?

All he had. Some editions inclose these words in a parenthesis. Gray's MS. gives it as in the text.

124 What is the object of *wish'd* ?

The third and fourth lines of this stanza respectively explain the first and second.

126 Draw, an infinitive in the same construction as *disclose*, which is adverbial to *seek*. This is evident from the first MS. draft in which Gray wrote:

"No farther seek his merits to disclose,
Nor seek to draw them from their dread abode."

Mitford would have it *Nor draw*. *Draw* would then be an imperative, co-ordinate with *seek*.

Dread abode. This is amplified and explained by the last line.

127 Alike, an adverb qualifying *repose.*

In trembling hope. Gray himself refers to Petrarch, *Sonnet,* 104: "*Paventosa speme.*"

Cf. Lucan, *Pharsalia*, VII. 297: "*Spe trepida.*"

Mallet, *Funeral Hymn,* 473:

"With trembling tenderness of hope and fear."

Beaumont, *Psyche,* XV. 314:

"Divided here 'twixt trembling hope and fear."

QUESTIONS FOR EXAMINATION.

THE TRAVELLER.

1 Sketch the plan of the *Traveller*.

2 What is its nominal object, and how far is that object attained?

3 What poet did G. imitate in the form of his poetry?

4 What poet took G. for his model, and how far was he successful in imitating him? What poems did he write in imitation?

5 To what variety of poetry does the *Traveller* belong? Make a list of poems belonging to this variety, with authors and dates.

6 Write a brief sketch of the person to whom the *Traveller* is dedicated.

7 What change took place, during the age of Johnson, in the method by which authors introduced their works to the public?

8 Quote the lines containing the thesis which the poet sets out to prove.

9 Contrast after G. the 'blessings' of 'nature' and 'art.'

10 Discuss the opinions advanced in ll. 91-92.

11 Write a synopsis of ll. 1-98.

12 Explain *heart untravelled, fleeting good, hundred realms, l. 41, his gods, patriot's boast, this favorite good, these truths.*

13 Reproduce in your own language G.'s description of Italy and the Italians. How far is his description correct? How far was his delineation of the character of the inhabitants just, when he wrote? How far does it apply at present?

14 Compare the *real* products of Italy with those mentioned by G. in his description.

15 What were the causes of the decline of Italian commerce?

16 What nations have successively controlled the commerce of Europe?

17 Define *assonance* and quote couplets which are examples of it.

QUESTIONS FOR EXAMINATION.

18 Quote lines containing examples of alliteration.

19 Whence was alliteration introduced into modern English?

20 Who were the leading painters, sculptors, and architects of the period of the revival of art in Italy?

21 Name and locate the chief commercial cities of mediæval Italy. In what did their commerce consist, and with whom was it carried on?

22 What story is connected with the writing of ll. 153-4?

23 Write brief notes on *gelid wings, pregnant quarry, plethoric ill, stormy mansion, struggling savage, finer joy, gentler morals.*

24 Criticise the description of the climate, physical features, and productions of Switzerland.

25 Give in your own language the substance of G.'s reasoning about the inhabitants of "barren States," and examine the correctness of his conclusions.

26 Why has the poet depreciated the climate and productions of Switzerland?

27 What would you infer as to G.'s appreciation of the sublime in nature, from his description of Swiss scenery?

28 Point out the finer touches in the delineation of the French character.

29 Quote any lines which specially exhibit G.'s *(a)* humor, *(b)* power of description.

30 Criticise the reasoning in ll. 269-280.

31 What peculiarity of the poetry of the eighteenth century is seen in ll. 273-280?

32 Point out any particulars in which G. has unjust y censured the French, and make what additions seem necessary to a complete description of the French character.

33 Make a list of leading French authors of G.'s time, and characterize their influence upon subsequent European thought and action.

34 Point out the particulars in which G. is unjust to the Dutch.

35 Refer to historical events in proof of the bravery and patriotism of the Dutch.

36 Quote some of the happier expressions used in the description of Holland.

37 What are "those ills" referred to in l. 302?

38 Tell what you know of the canals and dykes of Holland.

39 Name the principal lakes of Holland.

QUESTIONS FOR EXAMINATION. 131

40 Examine the relationship existing between the ancestors of the Dutch and English.

41 Draw a diagram of the Teutonic languages, shewing clearly how the English and Dutch are related.

42 Quote lines which contain allusions to the poet's personal history.

43 Characterize G.'s description of the climate, scenery, and inhabitants of Britain.

44 Compare the description of the peasantry in the different countries described.

45 If l. 333 be taken to mean that the English peasant exercised the right of franchise, how far is it correct?

46 Mention the different Acts by which the franchise has since been extended.

47 What "ills" are represented as arising in England from freedom?

48 Explain the historical allusions in ll. 345-6.

49 Compare the injurious effects of wealth upon the English and the Dutch, according to the poet.

50 What other writer has predicted a fate similar to that depicted in ll. 359-360?

51 Illustrate ll. 356, 358 by prominent examples.

52 Quote the apostrophe to Freedom.

53 Mention the leading periodicals of G.'s time, specifying those to which he contributed.

54 Give the names of the nine original members of the Literary Club.

55 What was G.'s relation to the Johnsonian circle?

56 Examine the statements made in ll. 373-6.

57 What events of the time, probably, suggested to the poet the opinions expressed in ll. 381-5?

58 Sketch the attempts of George III. to render the kingly power supreme.

59 Cite, from English history, instances illustrating l. 394.

60 In what sense is the king said to be the 'source of honor'?

61 Quote the lines that were written by Dr. Johnson.

62 Sketch the prevalent tendencies of G.'s age from a literary and from a political standpoint.

63 Quote the part of the *Traveller* which forms the text for the *Deserted Vi"age*.

64 To what extent is this poem a reflex of the sentiments and mode of expression of Dr. Johnson?

65 What title did Dr. Johnson propose for the *Traveller?*

66 Quote the lines containing the conclusion at which the poet professes to arrive.

67 Point out all deviations from strict grammatical construction in the *Traveller.*

68 To what school of poetry does G. belong?

69 What variety of poetry was prevalent during the eighteenth century?

70 Who were the leading actors, dramatists, poets, novelists, and historians of G.'s age?

71 How many editions of the *Traveller* were published during the poet's lifetime?

72 "No other poems from Gray's *Odes* to Cowper's *Table-Talk* can be said to have lived." What poems are referred to?

73 What reasons had G. for thinking that the *Traveller* would not meet with popular approval?

74 Make a list of G.'s poetical and prose works.

75 Give the history of the production of the *Traveller*, and point out the influence of its publication upon G.'s social standing.

76 How was the *Traveller* introduced to public notice?

77 Name G.'s dramatic works and characterize them.

78 What are the different varieties of poetry?

79 When was rhyme introduced into English poetry?

80 Select lines beginning with trochees or spondees.

81 Who were the poets-laureate during the life of G.?

82 What poet was most popular in fashionable circles when G. wrote?

83 What is the chief charm of G.'s style?

84 Give an account of English politics during the last ten years of G.'s life.

85 Illustrate from the *Traveller* any of the defects of G.'s style.

86 Write notes on the proper names in the poem.

87 What, according to the poet, is the 'favorite good" of the different nations reviewed?

88 Trace the changes in G.'s social position, from his attendance upon the 'beggars of Axe Lane,' till he became intimate with the chief literary men of his time,

QUESTIONS FOR EXAMINATION.

89 Give an account of the condition of poets and poetry during the age of G.

90 Sketch the life of the great political economist of this period, and state in what respects the poet's theories conflict with those advanced by this great writer.

91 What contemporary poet made poetry a vehicle for political warfare?

92 What two great moralities are inculcated in this poem?

93 Mention the different schools at which G. received his education.

94 Name the successive occupations in which G. was engaged during his life.

95 Which was the first novel of English domestic life? Characterize it.

96 Who have written biographies of G.?

97 What are the leading characteristics of the dramatic literature of this period?

98 Trace the influence of the publication of Percy's *Reliques*, upon poetical literature.

99 Account for the popularity of the rhyming couplet. Name leading poems in which it is employed, and point out to what variety of poetry it is best adapted.

100 To what extent are the following lines from the pen of Garrick a correct delineation of the character of G.?

" Here, Hermes, says Jove, who with nectar was mellow,
Go fetch me some clay—I will make an odd fellow:
Right and wrong shall be jumbled, much gold and some dross,
Without cause be he pleased, without cause be he cross;
Be sure, as I work, to throw in contradictions,
A great love of truth, yet a mind turn'd to fictions;
Now mix these ingredients, which, warm'd in the baking,
Turn'd to *learning* and *gaming, religion* and *raking.*
With the love of a wench, let his writings be chaste;
Tip his tongue with strange matter, his lips with fine taste
That the rake and the poet o'er all may prevail,
Set fire to the head and set fire to the tail;
For the joy of each sex on the world I'll bestow it,
This scholar, rake, Christian, dupe, gamester, and poet.
Though a mixture so odd, he shall merit great fame,
And among brother mortals be Goldsmith his name;
When on earth this strange meteor no more shall appear,
You, Hermes, shall fetch him, to make us sport here."

THE ELEGY.

1 Where was the *Elegy* written?
2 What are the leading thoughts contained in it?
3 What constitutes the peculiar charm of the poem?
4 Describe the metre. What other poems prior to the *Elegy* were written in similar quatrains?
✓5 What is an Elegy? Make a list of Elegiac poems, with dates and authors.
6 Distinguish Elegy, Epitaph and Dirge.
7 Sketch the history of the production of the *Elegy*.
8 Give a chronological list of Gray's works.
9 Write a sketch of the life of the person who exercised the greatest influence on literature, during the eighteenth century.
10 Give a history of the curfew in England, and state meaning of this word in the first line.
11 Compare the power of description of Gray and Goldsmith, illustrating by passages from the *Traveller* and *Elegy*.
12 In l. 6, what is the subject of *holds*? Why?
13 *Save*, l. 7. Give the history of this word. Similar words.
14 What is meant by *lowly bed* in l. 20?
15 Quote examples of alliteration and imperfect rhyme. What are the requirements of perfect rhyme?
16 Derive *curfew, lea, landscape, solemn, tinklings, ancient, clarion*.
17 Explain *parting*, l. 5, *droning flight, ivy-mantled, secret, rude*, l. 17, *echoing horn*.
18 How many editions of the *Elegy* were published during the author's lifetime? Into what languages has it been translated?
19 Give the substance of G.'s criticism of Gray, published in the *Monthly Review*.
20 Explain *stubborn glebe, ambition, grandeur, boast of heraldry, trophies, long-drawn aisle*.
21 Write a note on Heraldry.
22 With what incident in Canadian history is l. 36 inseparably connected?
23 Derive *sire, stubborn, ambition, poor, pomp, beauty, trophies, fretted, anthem, vault*.

QUESTIONS FOR EXAMINATION. 135

24 Quote Dr. Johnson's opinion of the *Elegy*, and criticize it.

25 Relate the circumstances attending its publication.

26 Sketch the part taken by Hampden in the defence of English liberty.

27 *Village Hampden.* Why *village?*

28 Give an account of Milton, and his writings.

29 *Mute inglorious Milton.* In your opinion would it be possible for a person possessing such a mind to remain in obscurity? Why?

30 Write an outline of Cromwell's life and character.

31 In l. 60, Gray implies that Cromwell was guilty *of his country's blood.* What is your opinion? Advance reasons in support of your position.

32 Write notes on *storied urn, animated bust, honor's voice, neglected spot, living lyre, spoils of Time, rage,* l. 52, *purest ray serene, little tyrant.*

33 State in your own words the meaning of sta. 14.

34 What church-yards claim the honor of having been the scene of the *Elegy?*

35 What are the leading characteristics of Gray's poetical and prose writings?

36 What reasons have been advanced for Johnson's contempt of Gray's productions?

37 Who were the leading parliamentary orators about the time of the writing of the *Elegy?*

38 Quote examples from English History illustrative of l. 67.

39 Refer to instances of the fulsome flattery of the dedications of the eighteenth century.

40 Quote from other poets, expressions depreciatory of trade, similar to that in l. 73.

41 Mention the Muses, with the province of literature assigned to each.

42 Explain ll. 61-64, *growing virtues,* l. 63, *Muse's flame, madding, these bones, passing tribute of a sigh, unletter'd muse, rustic moralist.*

43 Derive *alone, mercy, frail, uncouth, elegy, text, moralist.*

44 Explain the origin of the custom of interring in the churchyard.

45 Mention English poets who are distinguished for high culture.

46 What is the grammatical construction in ll. 85, 86?

47 Repeat sta. 23, and point out its beauties.

48 *For thee.* In what other poems does Gray refer to himself?

49 *Babbles.* Quote other examples of onomatopoetic words.

50 Explain *warm precincts, pious drops, wonted fires, upland lawn.*

51 Whom did Gray profess to adopt as his model?

52 Point out every allusion in this poem to events of the time and condition of the people.

53 What was the state of education among the masses in Gray's time?

54 Give the synonyms of *lay* in l. 115, and criticise its use there.

55 Repeat from memory, the Epitaph with which the *Elegy* closes.

56 Discuss the grammatical construction of ll. 117, 118.

57 Is this Epitaph a correct delineation of the character of the person for whom it was intended? Give your reasons.

58 How can his *frailties* be said to have *their dread abode* in *the bosom of his Father and his God?*

59 Explain *another came, church-way,* l. 119, *dread abode,* l. 128.

60 Point out and criticise all deviations from grammatical accuracy in this poem.

61 Point out all peculiarities in the scansion.

62 Select examples of the most prominent figures of speech n the *Elegy.* Would you consider the poem overloaded with igures?

63 Quote any parallel passages from the *Traveller* and *Elegy.*

64 Contrast G. and Gray as poets, and as prose writers.

65 Dr. Johnson has called Gray a 'mechanical poet.' Ex-mine this statement.

66 Tell what you know of Gray's intimate friends.

67 Draw up series of contrasts between G. and Gray, *(a)* as to their lives, *(b)* their character, *(c)* their culture.

68 What evidences of Gray's extensive reading are seen in his *Elegy?*

69 What were the different studies to which Gray devoted his attention?

70 To whom are we chiefly indebted for the particulars of Gray's life?

71 What was Gray's opinion of Goldsmith?

72 What objection was at first urged against Gray's poetry?

73 What tribute has Gray paid to Walpole's statesmanship, in the *Elegy?*

74 Examine the force of the objections advanced by Wordsworth against Gray's poetry.

75 Specify the chief changes and alterations made in the *Elegy* after the publication of the first edition.

FINIS.

www.ingramcontent.com/pod-product-compliance
Lightning Source LLC
Chambersburg PA
CBHW030331170426
43202CB00010B/1093